PRINCIPLES

OF

PRAYER

© 2006 A.D – PRINCIPLES OF PRAYER
Dr. D.K. Olukoya
ISBN: 978-8021-66-2
A Publication of
TRACTS AND PUBLICATIONS GROUP
MOUNTAIN OF FIRE AND MIRACLES MINISTRIES
13, Olasimbo Street, off Olumo Road, (By UNILAG Second Gate),
Onike, Iwaya.
P.O.Box 2990, Sabo, Yaba, Lagos, Nigeria. 01-867439,
4704267,4704367
Website: www.mountain-of-fire.com
E-mail: mfmhqworldwide@mountainoffire.org

First Edition

Table of Contents

CHAPTER ONE
FACTS ABOUT PRAYER

The subject of prayer is very wide and deep. It has been said that prayer is one of the three pillars that uphold a Christian. The other two pillars are holiness and the word of God. You cannot become a heaven-bound Christian if you fail in any of these three pillars. If you do not study and meditate upon the word of God, or live a holy and prayerful life, then, you have a big problem. The three must go together.

Many things have been said about prayer. You can come across some in my other books. We have been told that prayer is the key in the hands of faith to open the doors of blessings. Our old Pentecostal fathers used to tell us that prayer is the staff to walk with God and to confront the enemy. Prayer is the only thing that the devil cannot offer, while a Christian is greatest on his knees.

Genesis 4: 25-26 tells us when prayer began in the history of mankind. It started from the family of Seth, the chosen generation. You may now ask the question: What is prayer?

- Prayer is conversation with God; that is, talking with your Creator.
- Prayer is offering your heart's desire unto God in the name of our Lord Jesus Christ, by the help of the Holy Spirit. The Bible states that we know not how or what we should pray, but that the Spirit Himself makes intercession for us in groaning that cannot be uttered. That is why it has to be done by the help of the Holy Spirit **(Romans 8: 26)**.
- Prayer is the rail on which the locomotion of God's power moves.
- Prayer is the gateway to God's presence.

- Prayer is a love affair with God.
- Prayer is the deepest expression of the soul.
- Prayer is talking to God and listening to Him speak to you.

Blessed is the man who would be silent enough to allow God to speak after he has spoken to Him. Blessed is the woman also that would be silent enough to listen to God speak to her after she has spoken to Him.

- Prayer is a two-way communication. It is the same as a telephone conversation. You speak from one end while someone listens at the other end. And when it is necessary, the person at the other end speaks too. Both of you speak and listen to each other in turns.

- Prayer is talking with the Almighty God, while He listens and also talks to you.

- What it does and where it stands could also illustrate prayer.

- Prayer is the greatest privilege of a redeemed soul.

- Prayer is getting direct access to the throne of God Almighty.

- Prayer is a weapon in the hour of conflict.

- Prayer is a defence in the moment of peril.

- It is a retreat in the season of exhaustion.

- Prayer is the mightiest force in the universe.

- Prayer is the key of the morning and the bolt of the night.

- Prayer takes the highest energy that a human being is capable of generating.

- Prayer is the most important work on earth.

- It is the greatest outlet of power.

- It is the wealth of poverty.

- It is the light of darkness.

- Prayer is the channel of God's grace.
- Prayer is the perpetual force against all powers of darkness in all their ramifications.
- Prayer is acting with God in His battle against evil.
- Prayer is spiritual bombing.
- Prayer unites the soul of man to God.
- It breaks down every opposing wall.
- It demolishes every fortress of hell.
- It is asking God to work in your life.
- Prayer is an act of love.
- Prayer succeeds when all other things fail.
- Prayer is spiritual sanitation.
- Prayer is omnipotent because it moves the hand that moves the world.
- Prayer is the hand that strikes down satan and his cohorts with all their evil devices.
- It releases God's divine energy.

THE PRINCIPLES OF ANSWERED PRAYERS

There are two major passages in the Bible that show that certain principles have to be observed before a prayer is speedily answered. If these principles are not followed, the outcome becomes unfavourable.

In the book of James we see a wonderful fact about prayer. **James 5:16** says, "The effectual fervent prayer of a righteous man availeth much." This means that a man can be effectual, fervent and righteous. If the word 'effectual' is removed from the statement, it becomes the fervent prayer of a righteous person. This means that a righteous man can pray fervent prayers that are not effectual. Secondly, the word 'effectual' indicates that a man can pray effectual prayers that are not fervent. Also, if the word righteous is removed, nothing happens. It means that all these three must work hand in hand. Prayer has to be effective, fervent and must be offered by a righteous man or woman for it to be answered. That is, it would avail. It would be successful.

When I was a young Christian, this verse of the Bible used to bother me a lot. It caused me some restlessness. I used to say to myself, "You see that Elijah was a man like you. He prayed that there should be no rain in the land and it came to pass." This single feat of Elijah challenged me a lot in those days. Elijah's prayer was answered because he strictly followed the principles given in the verse above. It is very easy for a man of God to stand on the pulpit, stretch forth his hands and pray for the entire congregation for thirty minutes or more. Yes, God would honour it and things would begin to happen. But such a man of God is not helping members of his church because he is not training them. There is an adage that says, "Give a man a piece of fish, you give him a meal; but teach him how to fish, and you have fed him for life." You may be somewhere and find nobody to pray for you, and if you do not know what to do, you would be in trouble. You must be able to do it yourself, anytime, anywhere. When you pray to the level you are supposed to, you would need no prophet or pastor to see visions for you, because you would have become a prophet yourself.

The Bible says that the effectual, fervent prayer of a righteous man avails much. It means that your prayer must be focused and fervent in order to move the hands of the Almighty. Another thing to consider is the word "righteous." For a man to get an answer to his prayer, he should not only be effectual or fervent, he must also be righteous. He must be holy within and without; in his thoughts, words and deeds.

Perhaps you pray fervently, yet your prayers do not avail much. You are puzzled and wonder why you always obtain very little results from your prayers. You are puzzled that God does not speak to you or instruct you on the steps to take or the way to go. The answer is simply lack of understanding of the principles of prayer. For prayer to be effective, it has to be fervent and said by a righteous man.

The principles of prayer were given by our Lord Jesus Christ Himself in what is commonly known as the "Lord's prayer" (Matthew 6: 9-15). Four different principles could be seen in our Lord's prayer. The first one is worship. It says, "Our Father which art in heaven, hallowed be thy name." The second one is the confirmation of God's will. The third one is request for daily provision and the fourth and last one is request for forgiveness. These are the steps or principles embedded in Jesus' prayer.

When we bring the principles highlighted in James 5: 16 and Matthew 6: 9-15 together, we would have standard principles that would serve as a base for answered prayers. These principles are:

1. **Praise and thanksgiving:** These two serve as the New Testament incense. In the Old Testament, incense was needed for worship. The word incense came from the Hebrew word "quota" which means fumigation, that is, evacuating or driving out unwanted occupants. Today, for you to pray effectively and worship God in spirit, you must offer the New Testament incense, which would in turn chase out other occupants. Once these other occupants are chased out, you can walk up to God and flow with Him.

Man is filled with his own devices, imaginations, doctrines and fears. Many a time, we take these into our prayers. This approach makes heaven to become closed. Someone who is praying with worry or anxiety about academics, husband, wife, armed robbers, visa, business etc would be distracted by them, and his prayer would not have a good effect. Therefore, you must first of all carry out a fumigation exercise, just like in the past, when people chased out rats by directing smoke into their holes. Once this is done in your life, you can flow with God without hindrance.

The effect of the exercise of praise and thanksgiving begins with you. It first purges your spirit, soul and body and goes forth to hallow God in heaven.

2. True worship: A true worshipper can ascend to God in heaven as he keeps his mind focused on Him. John 4: 24 describes the true worshippers as those who worship God in spirit and in truth. The Lord Almighty says He would seek those who worship Him in spirit and in truth. It is a great privilege to be sought by God. Therefore, leave your worries behind, concentrate and worship God with the whole of your heart and He will give you His attention. Moses understood the principle of staying focused, so, he said to the Israelites: "Stand still and see the salvation of the Lord." This issue deals with the heart. Our heart must be still and focused to connect to God.

Some people begin their prayers by telling God how terrible things have been for them. They lament and sob to show how terribly affected they have been. If you start your prayer like this, it would not affect or move God in any way, rather it would strengthen your enemy more against you. Do not tell God how great your problems are, but tell your problems how great your God is. Do not look at Goliath and scream. Rather, say and believe that you will not miss your target once you throw your stone.

God called David a man after His own heart, and David himself gave praises to Him in Psalm 100:4. David was a great man and a winner because his prayers were scented with incense, which is praise. Therefore, you must enter into the presence of the Lord with thanks and praises. Leave your troubles behind, open your heart unto the Lord, and enter into His gates with thanksgiving. Start every prayer with thanksgiving not because all you will request of the Lord are already yours, but because your name is written in the book of life, which cannot be exchanged for anything. Any request you make is secondary to thanksgiving and praises. When you want to pray at home, do not begin

6

your thanksgiving to God with warfare songs. Rather, start with the incense, which is thanksgiving and praise. God has been good to you and you need to tell Him so.

Paul the Apostle was a winner, champion and conqueror. If you ask him how you would be able to light the spiritual incense, what he would likely say is: "Give thanks!" He gave thanks while inside the prison, after he had been terribly battered and dragged on the ground from the market place to prison and with all his body full of bruises. At this point in his life, Paul had a very good reason to abuse God if he had wanted to do so: after all, he was on his own when God called and asked him to go to Macedonia. Yet, look at what happened to him. He should have sat down and said to God: "See what is happening to me. After all, I did not call myself but you called me. Did you call me to be battered like this? Is this fair?" Paul might have been right to say all this, but he did not. Rather he gave thanks to the Almighty.

The same Apostle Paul suffered a shipwreck. For three weeks all the people in the ship never saw the light. The whole place was in disarray and Paul started thanking God. So, when you give thanks, your unfavourable circumstances would change for the better. Praises drive out doubts, grumbling, murmurings and complaints. Then you would begin to hear from heaven. **Revelation 8: 3-4** says, "And another angel came and stood at the altar, having a golden censer; and there was given unto him much incense, that he should offer it with the prayers of all saints upon the golden altar which was before the throne. And the smoke of the incense, which came with the prayers of the saints, ascended up before God out of the angel's hand."

You can now see that incense is something that should accompany your prayers. The Bible says we should be careful for nothing: but in everything, by prayer and thanksgiving, let our request be made known unto God (Philippians 4:6).

3. Confirmation of God's will: This third principle cannot be shoved aside if one must get answers to his prayers. Before you start praying, always confirm God's will concerning your request. **Ephesians 5:17** says, "Wherefore be ye not unwise, but understanding what the will of the Lord is."

You need to find out whether what you are asking for is in line with God's will for your life. Once you confirm that, you can ask for it in prayer. If a thing is not God's will for you, as a child of God, He will not give it to you. If you do not know what God wants for you and what He would permit you to get, your prayer would be as that of one beating the air. For instance, you should not go to God asking Him to allow you to marry the second wife. Of course, that is not God's will for your life and He will not give you an answer to it.

Pursuing the will of God requires complete submission to God. Your motive for any request you make unto God is what determines the answer. If your motive is wrong, or you lack complete submission, you will not have an answer. Praying in line with God's will for you brings quick response to your prayer.

4. Identify your need and be specific: Isaiah 41:21 says, "Produce your cause, saith the Lord; bring forth your strong reasons, saith the King of Jacob." Your needs must be identified and specific. I discovered that what many people want is not what they need. Somebody, who is asking God to make him rich, while he promises to sponsor the work of God to any level, may not need to be rich after all. May be all that he needs is for God to turn his life upside down and drain all impurities in his life to make him useful. But he is asking to be very rich.

Another person might say, "O God, I want to be prophesying and seeing visions so that people would be praising God for my life." That is what he wants, but his need may be that the spirit of anger in his life should die. Somebody who still has anger and would not face it and root it out should not be asking for spiritual gifts because they are not meant for people like him. Such a person is asking for what he wants and not what he needs. Being specific means that when you are asking God for a husband you should specify what kind of husband you want. If you want a wife, what kind of wife do you want? You must be specific because there are so many men but very few husbands, and likewise, so many women but very few wives.

Blind Bartimaeus prayed an unspecific prayer: "Jesus, thou Son of David, have mercy on me." He cried out to Jesus in anguish yet he did not make any specific point in his cry. He asked for "mercy" but there are so many mercies in the Bible. Jesus was even helpless, though His attention was captured. He had to ask Bartimaeus what he really wanted. And he answered and said, "That I may receive my sight." He now spoke specifically. Avoid embarking on fruitless prayers. You may pray for two hours without making any impact on God until you become specific. For example, if you want deliverance, what areas and deliverance from what? Be specific, hit the target, then answers will follow.

5. Back up your prayers with the Scriptures: Isaiah 43: 26 says, "Put me in remembrance: let us plead together: declare thou, that thou mayest be justified." After confirming God's will for your life, ask whatever you desire according to that will by being specific. Then back it up with the word of God. When you use God's word for Him, He doesn't delay but acts immediately because it is His word, He must act it. He says we should remind Him of His own words.

There are about 7,487 promises in the Bible. You must identify the one you want, then tell God, "You promised to do this, do it for me." Once it is His will for you, He would not hesitate to do it. The scripture is the springboard you need to stand on to claim what you need. Gather them together, meditate upon them, and make sure they become part and parcel of your life. Our old Pentecostal fathers were fond of reciting Psalms. They cleverly memorised the word of God and applied any portion of it to their specific situations. It is very sad that the number of people interested in memorising the scriptures is declining day by day. Many people think that memorising the scriptures is for Sunday school children only. It would help you as a Bible believer to have a lot of scriptures in your memory. Jesus was able to counter the attack of the devil by quoting the scriptures He had in his memory. He often said, "It is written..." Once your prayers are backed up with and by scriptures, the answers manifest quickly.

6. Pray with faith and an expectant heart: James 1: 5-8 says, "If any of you lack wisdom, let him ask of God, that giveth to all men liberally, and upbraideth not; and it shall be given him. But let him ask in faith, nothing wavering. For he that wavereth is like a wave of the sea driven with the wind and tossed. For let not that man think that he shall receive any thing of the Lord. A double minded man is unstable in all his ways."

Whatever you ask outside faith cannot be given, no matter how specific or how many scriptures you quote. You need to believe absolutely that what you are requesting from God can be given or done by Him. Mark 11:24, which is the word of our Lord Jesus Christ Himself buttresses this point. It says: "Believe and ye shall find."

The second part of the sixth principle states that one should be expectant. This aids your faith, because it drives out doubt. Once you begin your prayer, believe that what you are asking for would be given to you. Then be in high expectation of that thing.

7. Present your case systematically before God: Do not pray vagabond prayers. Ask for one thing at a time. Do not pray: "O Lord, thank you for keeping and saving me from flesh eaters. I ask that you lay your hands upon me and that my work should prosper. I pray for our church. I pray that my pastor will live long and grow old. I also pray for my town and village, in Jesus' name." This is nothing but a vagabond prayer. It has no focus.

A good prayer warrior takes up a prayer point and prays it to a level of assurance before moving to the next one. In fact, as he prays, he feels the assurance of answers. One of the best examples in the Bible that buttresses this principle is the conversation between Abraham and God. Three men visited Abraham and were well entertained. Later, they told Abraham about their mission: "We have come to destroy Sodom and Gomorrah but it would be unfair if we do it without informing you." Abraham quickly did a little bit of mathematics: Lot was there with his wife, daughters and sons-in-law. He now said: "Far be it from you, O Lord, that you would destroy the righteous with the unrighteous." God answered and said: "All right, if I find just 50 righteous men in the city, I will leave it." Abraham now said, "Lord, supposing you find 40 righteous people, will you still destroy the city?" God gave a positive answer. And Abraham said, "O God, do not be angry, what about 30 people?" God said He would not destroy the city if He found 30 righteous men and women. Abraham was targeting 10 people. Why? There were Lot, his wife and two unmarried daughters at home as well as three married daughters and their husbands, bringing the total number of people to 10. Abraham was systematic in presenting his request. Learn to be systematic in your prayers and the result would be positive.

8. Do not be selfish in your prayer: James 4: 3 says, "Ye ask, and receive not, because ye ask amiss, that ye may consume it upon your lusts." A man came to us for prayer. He was doing very well until the powers of the emptier entered into his life. When he came, he prayed violently and his problem was over and suddenly we did not see him again. If the devil gets hold of this kind of person the second time, he would rarely survive. He would shout his voice hoarse praying and God would say: "Keep quiet, what did you do with the money I gave you at first? Did you bless me with it or squander it on yourself?"

9. Be serious with prayers: Prayer is warfare and not a joking matter. Talking with the Creator of heaven and earth is not a joking matter at all. The Bible even says we should come boldly to the throne of grace. This shows that it is actually a serious matter.

10. Do not dictate to God: Do not dictate or suggest to God how He should answer your prayers. Let Him do it His own way. Remember that He is God. Do not try to help Him answer your prayer. If you go through your Bible very carefully, you would see the various amazing ways that He answers prayers. .

At the Red Sea, Moses thought it was the end of the road, there was nothing more he could do. He called unto God and God said, "What is that in your hand? Was it not with this same rod that you battered all the gods of Egypt to submission? Was it not with this rod that you disgraced all the kings and princes of Egypt? Now use it." Moses used it and God disgraced the enemies. He parted the Red Sea and made way where there was no way. This single act is one of the greatest miracles in the Bible.

God told the children of Israel to march round the wall of Jericho seven times. This they did and the wall fell flat. If they had tried to help God, it would not have happened the way it did. Do not try to help God, because you will get into more trouble if you do. **John 4: 46-53** says, "So Jesus came again into Cana of Galilee, where he made the water wine. And there was a certain nobleman, whose son was sick at Capernaum. When he heard that Jesus was come out of Judaea into Galilee, he went unto him, and besought him that he would come down, and heal his son: for he was at the point of death. Then said Jesus unto him, Except ye see signs and wonders, ye will not believe. The nobleman saith unto him, Sir, come down ere my child die. Jesus saith unto him, Go thy way; thy son liveth. And the man believed the word that Jesus had spoken unto him, and he went his way. And as he was now going down, his servants met him, and told him, saying, Thy son liveth. Then enquired he of them the hour when he began to amend. And they said unto him, Yesterday at the seventh hour the fever left him. So the father knew that it was at the same hour, in which Jesus said unto him, Thy son liveth: and himself believed, and his whole house."

Once the word of God comes forth, receive it wholly without question. Sometimes, a word of knowledge might come for a particular person and other people who are very clever would tap from its overflow. They can even claim it faster than the person it is meant for can.

When we try to dictate to God how He should answer our prayers, we restrict Him. One thing we fail to understand is the wonderful aspect of the Father described by Isaiah. He described Him as wonder. The word 'wonder' denotes beyond imagination, unexpected, unimaginable, unusual, etc. We cannot actually say this is how God is going to do something, yet we know He is going to do it. The earlier we realise this, the easier it is for us to flow with Him and expect our prayers to be answered. He often feels disappointed about the way we try to predict Him. Often times, we feel that our prayer has not been answered because we do not see it the way we have expected

11. Your prayer must be persistent: God's delay is not God's denial. Each day brings you closer to the realisation of your dreams. Deuteronomy 3:25-26 says, "I pray thee, let me go over, and see the good land that is beyond Jordan, that goodly mountain, and Lebanon. But the Lord was wroth with me for your sakes, and would not hear me: and the Lord said unto me, Let it suffice thee; speak no more unto me of this matter." What is this passage saying? It is saying, "Shut up. Do not pray that prayer again." You must pray persistently like that man who refused to give up, while knocking on his friend's door. "We want food, we want food! We are dying in my house. We are starving to death," he said. Despite the cold shoulders he got from his friend, he persisted with

the knocking and eventually, it paid off. This is how prayers should be said.

It is not that God is difficult to approach, or hard to convince, that is why prayer is hard but because of the powers of hindrance in the second heaven; the satanic angels that are fighting Christians day and night. This is why we say prayer is a battle. Look at blind Bartimaeus, he refused to stop crying. It was the same with the widow in Jesus' parable. She kept harassing and pestering the judge until the man gave in. What about the woman who wanted Jesus to heal her sick daughter? She harassed Jesus until she got what she wanted.

Most of the prayers in both the Old and New Testaments could be seen as holy cries: "O God, You must do what you have said." This is the prayer of those who must get an answer. And one beautiful thing about God is that He never discourages anybody. All He wants is for you to ask because His word is "Yea and Amen." You can always be sure that every discouragement and distraction in prayer is from the devil. He could pinch your body or make your child to cry so that you would be distracted and cannot pray. He does the same thing to the dog and makes it bark all night to disrupt your prayer. He causes both husband and wife to be angry with each other.

12. Pray to the level of assurance: You must pray to a level of assurance and begin to praise God for the answer. If you pray and doubt is still in your heart, it means that you have not reached the level of assurance. A Christian that is always in tune with the Holy Ghost should pray to this level and confirm that surely the case is settled.

Sometime ago, I was listening to a white preacher on television. He was talking about faith in prayer. He said that once you ask God for something, He gives it to you, and you receive it immediately. Therefore, you need not ask Him again. He was wrong because he did not understand that God can pour out His blessings but some forces such as household wickedness would say, "No! He would not get it." But as long as God is concerned, He has poured out His blessings and from that point battle begins. This was exactly the case with Daniel. God answered his prayer instantly but the answer could not get to him because of the wicked spirit stopping it. He did not stop praying until he got the answer (Daniel 10:2-6, 11-13). Therefore, do not stop praying until you witness certain assurance in you consciousness.

ESSENTIALS OF PRAYER

By essentials of prayer I mean the ingredients required for true prayer.

1. Prayers must involve the whole of your being: Your spirit, soul and body have to be fully involved in the praying exercise, since the outcome of an answered prayer affects the entire man. The greatest result of prayer comes to the person who gives all of himself and all that belongs to him to God. It is the secret of full consecration. This is a condition for successful praying. It brings the largest fruit.

God needs all that exist in a man to answer his prayer. He needs a whole-hearted and consecrated man through whom He can exercise and make manifest His purposes and plans concerning men. A man whose mind wanders about has not started the walk to the mountain of answered prayers. Your imagination and thought must be involved in your prayer. You cannot pray effectively with a wandering mind. Your prayer cannot be effective while your mind is on your problems or on an appointment you must keep. Your imagination too must be put under control.

The trinity of man in prayer

Man consists of the spirit, soul and body. These three entities come together to form man. And for prayer to make an impact, they must all be united. The body engages in prayer when it assumes the right posture. The mind too has to be prepared to approach the throne of grace. True praying focuses on what your thoughts are. You must be able to hold unto a particular thing you would love to take to the Lord. "What shall I ask from God this hour?" After you have settled what to request for, the very first step, which is a mental one, has to be taken.

Your mind should totally be given over to God, thinking of Him, what is needed for that hour and what has been received in the past.

In 1Timothy 2: 8 Paul buttresses this point: "I will therefore that men pray every where, lifting up holy hands, without wrath and doubting." For you to have your possessions, which you have been deprived of for sometime, you have to involve your whole being in prayer. To break any evil curse upon your life, the whole of you must pray. Divine power from on high does not come when the mind is troubled or when you are praying with divided attention. You have to be focused and serious and pray with all concentration. Our Lord Jesus prayed with His whole being in Gethsemane. He had a particular prayer point that He repeated: "O my Father, let this cup pass..." Luke 22: 41-45 says, "And he was withdrawn from them about a stone's cast, and kneeled down, and prayed. Saying, Father, if thou be willing, remove this cup from me: nevertheless not my will, but thine, be done. And there appeared an angel unto him from heaven, strengthening him. And being in an agony he prayed more earnestly: and his sweat was as it were great drops of blood falling down to the ground. And when he rose up from prayer, and was come to his disciples, he found them sleeping for sorrow."

No wonder He prayed earnestly. An angel was sent to strengthen Him. Before someone could pray to the level of bringing down an angel to minister to him, he must have involved his entire being. I encourage you to do likewise.

2. Humility of heart: This is another essential of prayer, which brings the praying soul near to God. It gives ready access to the throne of grace. Humility is of great value in the sight of God and you must have it if you must receive from Him. The Bible says, "God resisteth the proud, but giveth grace to the humble" (1 Peter 5: 5). This shows that once God resists you, He cannot answer your prayers. For Him to accept you, even while you approach His throne for one thing or the other, you have to be humble.

Humility means modesty, lowliness of the mind or having a low opinion of oneself. It means keeping away from the public gaze and not hunting for high places. It never exalts itself in the eyes of others no matter how highly placed. Humility enables one to gain access to God when other qualities fail. It may take the entire book to describe what humility is but its full description is seen in the lifestyle of our Lord Jesus Christ.

In the parable of the Pharisee and the publican, one could see how important the element of humility is in the place of prayer. The publican, who showed humility, was justified while the Pharisee was condemned for his high mindedness.

Humility is an indispensable requisite for true prayer. You may have achieved a lot for God, you may be known as a great prophet who performs all sorts of miracles, or you may feel that you are a righteous man that needs not ask for the forgiveness of sins. All these do not matter in the presence of God. If you pride yourself on your achievements and pray with that kind of heart, God will not listen to you.

Abraham showed humility when he was pleading for the righteous in Sodom and Gomorrah, and as a result, the anger of God was doused so that Abraham was able to ask Him more questions. Solomon also showed such humility to God. He abased his grandeur, glory and majesty and assumed the right attitude to God. He said: "I am but a little child, and know not how to go out or to come in." And God said to him, "Ask for any thing." It is rare for God to show such grace in such unlimited manner. What Solomon asked for at that moment was not denied him, but he was given more than he expected. Your prayer must move on the wings of humility into the presence of God.

For humility to be complete, every grievance and bitterness of the heart must be discarded before going to God in prayer. No matter how badly you might have been hurt, if your prayer must be answered, you must exercise forgiveness from the depth of your heart, the offence must be forgotten before you go to God.

CHAPTER TWO
PRAYER KILLERS

It has been earlier said that prayer is a spiritual exercise and not a physical one. It is a question of neither religion nor a psychological kind of something, but strictly a spiritual exercise. The Bible makes us to understand that God is a Spirit (John 4: 24, Hebrew 12:9). These scriptures tell us that God is the Father of spirits and anyone that has anything to do with Him must move to His realm – the spiritual realm.

Prayer is serious business and hard work. If it were a simple exercise, Jesus would not have prayed until His sweat was like drops of blood. As earlier said, prayer is a battle and the devil has various weapons he uses to stop people from praying. The devil and his agents are the prayer killers. A killer squeezes life out of someone. When we talk about dead people, we believe they are people who can neither talk nor relate with living things again. However, the Bible gives us a different picture of "the dead." In the Bible, we find people who are dead though living. Therefore, the prayer life of a person may be dead while the person is still praying. Most of the time, it becomes hard to pray when these killers have already taken the upper hand.

In 1977, two brothers were living in a room and praying very vigorously. After sometime, they noticed that they were suddenly dozing off because they were no longer able to pray before they slept. Even if they woke up at night to pray, they found that unlike in former times when they would pray for up to three hours non-stop, they could no longer pray for more than five minutes before sleeping off. When this type of thing begins to happen to a Christian, it means that his prayer temperature is going down. So, he should jump out quickly and do something fast because it means that danger is lurking around the corner. It means that something tragic is about to happen and he needs to wake up. If he allows the situation to go on like that and for one week he cannot pray very well for at least 30 minutes, but can spend 30 minutes arguing or quarrelling, or one hour dressing up before the mirror, then trouble would surely come from prayer killers.

These two brothers noticed that their prayer lives were going down, and one night one of them decided to take the bull by the horn and said: "Enough is enough. If this situation continues like this, very soon, there will be trouble in this place. Tonight, I will not sleep." And true to his word, he did not sleep. He started to pray, pacing up and down in their one-room apartment. He prayed till 1:30 a.m. when the Spirit of God said to him: "Son, I am going to show you something today, just continue praying." Prayer becomes sweeter when you begin to hear the Spirit of God talking to you because you would receive fresh energy. That is one of the secrets of prayer. You may start in a gentle manner, as if it would never catch fire. Something may even say to you, "Why don't you give up and go to bed." But as you persist, the anointing will fall on you and you will no longer feel like stopping. The anointing came upon this brother and God said to him, "Open your door and step outside." He did and was amazed at what he saw. It was one of his co-tenants, who used to sell bread and beans to them, tying a black thread around the house. The brother stood there in bewilderment, watching what the woman was doing. Of course, God made him invisible to the woman. While she was weaving the black thread round the house, she was muttering some words: "All right, you will see. You are already complaining that you can no longer pray as you used to. This one will eventually kill your prayer lives completely." She was putting the spirit of heaviness upon that house, so that they would be weighed down and can no longer pray. I pray that the activities of prayer killers would be exposed to you in detail so that you can take your stand and know where to face.

The activities of prayer killers are so much today that Christians pray only when they are in church. We all must wake up and wage war against these great agents of the devil who fight against the children of the Most High.

19

WHAT ARE PRAYER KILLERS?

1. Spirit of heaviness: This deadly spirit is like the infection that affects the area of the brain, which supplies strength and agility to the human system. It results in unexplainable weakness of the body. The spirit of heaviness weighs down a person and squeezes life out of him. It makes it impossible for a person to communicate with God as His child. It is a powerful killer. No wonder the Bible says, "He gave unto them beauty for ashes: the oil of joy for mourning, the garment of praise for the spirit of heaviness" (Isaiah 61:3). This means that the spirit of heaviness is a very powerful weapon that disallows many Christians from praying to the point of breakthroughs. God specifically told me that many Christians are candidates in the school of heaviness. The devil sits some people down, give them lectures that would weigh them down and discourage them. The devil would say, "How old are you? You are already 54. What have you achieved in life? Your contemporaries are managers all over the place. Your brother was one of the astronauts in the United States of America who visited the moon. Your younger sister got married before you, and you do not even have a single degree. You just sat down there singing useless songs." You would listen, and because he has your attention, he would ask further questions such as: "Tell me, how far have you gone now, even with all your education? What have you achieved all these years?" After listening to the devil's lecture, you would probably take a deep breath and begin to consider it. And as you do that, you become weighed down and discouraged, and gradually begin to withdraw from prayer until your prayer life finally dies. That is the trick of the devil. Beware! Do not be ignorant of the devices of the devil (2 Corinthians 2:11).

Beloved, know that as long as the devil is unable to kill your prayer life, he cannot catch you. But the moment he succeeds in squeezing life out of your prayers, his full operation begins. He would not say, "Do not pray." All he does is to squeeze life out of your prayers and render them ineffective. If you have once had a nice encounter with the Lord in prayer, you should know when your prayer is dead. And if you are in this kind of school, you must get out today. Jesus said, "Take no thought about tomorrow, for tomorrow will take care of itself, it is sufficient to deal with the evil of today." Therefore, do not carry today's problem into tomorrow. Yesterday is too late to worry about, while tomorrow is too early to worry about. What you have is now, today. Our confidence is that we do not fear what the future may bring, because the man who holds the future is our Father. He is the God of yesterday, today and forever. Why should I worry about my life when God Himself is in control?

2. Laziness: Ecclesiastes 10:18 says, "By much slothfulness the building decayeth; and through idleness of the hands the house droppeth through." We discover that spiritual laziness squeezes life out of a person's prayer life. There is nobody who would say that he loves to pray every time and everywhere. No! The flesh does not like prayer and you have to learn to be persistent.

Laziness is the direct product of the flesh which the devil uses against many giants in God's kingdom today. You need a breakthrough over your flesh which ever stands against prayer. When prayer becomes part of you, the flesh will have no space to hide. This is why you need to pray for the spirit of prayer. Prayer is a spirit that must baptise your life. Once you have the baptism of the spirit of prayer, prayer killers will not overcome you, no matter how hard they try.

Check how you manage your God-given precious 24 hours per day. If you still oversleep and waste part of this limited resource to gossip and wander around, laziness is already in your bosom. The things expected to be done for two days; do you still struggle to do them in four days? Some people are too lazy to pray up to 30 minutes in a day or study their Bible for 20 minutes. If they continue this way, it will be disastrous. The killer would take advantage of that to drag them behind God's schedule for them.

3. Carnal conversation: Some Christians are not able to tame their tongues against speaking in an unholy way. When you talk loosely, your prayer would lack power and life in it. In Psalms 34:13 and Proverbs 13: 3, we learn that loose talkers lack spiritual power. If unbelievers in your place are cracking unwholesome jokes, you as a believer should not join them. If you do, by the time you leave, they would make fun of you. They would say: "Ah, we did not know that his Christianity is not serious." Loose talkers lack spiritual power and when there is something serious to be done, nobody will approach a loose talker. People would go to that same fanatical brother they never liked, because they know within themselves that he is more likely to have the power to help them. As a man gets exhausted when he talks for hours so also a Christian pours out his spiritual energy when he talks too much and unnecessarily. Loose talk is a prayer killer. Avoid it now!

4. Overfeeding: Philippians 3:19 says, "Whose end is destruction, whose God is their belly, and whose glory is in their shame, who mind earthly things." This scripture talks about people whose god is their belly, people who overfeed themselves. 1 Corinthians 6:13 also reveals that those who eat too much can indeed never be prayer warriors, and this is the reason many people do not hear from God. They overfeed and oversleep. Some people are terribly scared of fasting and because they are so scared, the enemy takes advantage of this to attack and eventually kill their prayer life. Those who eat too much would not be able to experience the kind of anointing they deserve. Because the heavier the stomach, the less anointing upon it. When you are full, stop eating. Do not eat more than your system can contain, it kills the life of prayer.

5. Constant travelling: When somebody is always changing environments, for example, today, you are observing your quiet time in the airplane, the next day in a train, another day in a hotel, and so on, you cannot really have a constant prayer life. You may find yourself in an environment where the Spirit of God wants you to pray aloud, but you cannot because you are a visitor. When you travel a lot, you cannot find children of God to pray with you. This kills prayer life.

6. Too many activities: Any Christian that must live a victorious prayer life must avoid being engrossed in too many activities, no matter how important some of them seem to be. In fact, some Christians don't know that the devil can keep them too busy with activities, even with so-called church work that they rarely have time for themselves. Do not become a working machine that produces nothing. God does not encourage a round-the-clock church worker or minister, one who works at the expense of healthy spiritual life. The fact is that some of the works done by these kinds of people are not recognised by God and are therefore fruitless. They are not recognised because they are not done with understanding and most people do theirs to impress their church leaders. All these are fruitless hard work. Even Moses, the anointed prophet and recognised man of God was caught in these fruitless activities. Jethro, his father-in-law, had to call him and direct him aright.

The devil uses this strategy to kill the prayer lives of Christians. Beware, learn from this, and turn a new leaf before it is too late. Everything you do outside prayer is service but relationship with God supercedes service for Him. Despite the fact that people came to Jesus to be healed and to hear from Him, He still found time to be alone to pray. He separated Himself to seek the face of God. Every activity without prayer is fruitless. In Biology, two processes are involved in the human body: catabolism and anabolism. One involves the use of energy and the other builds up energy, but both must balance for life to continue. This also applies to spiritual matters.

7. Failure to observe spiritual retreat: Matthew 14:23 says, "And when he had sent the multitudes away, he went up into a mountain apart to pray: and when the evening was come, he was there alone."
When you do not observe a spiritual retreat, a time you spend apart to meet with God, life would be squeezed out of your prayer. If all you do is come to church and listen to music and dance and at home you sleep,

and refuse to observe your retreat, your prayer life will eventually be killed. Please, note that when I say retreat, I do not mean that you should embark on three to seven days retreat to meet with God. You can hold a fifteen or thirty minute retreat. It may be one hour or one to three days. You can do anything, but the most important thing is that you keep yourself apart to commune with God. It does not have to be done along with fasting, but use the opportunity to refill your spirit. It is a powerful exercise that energises your prayer life. Jesus was always doing it. He was fond of separating Himself from His disciples to go and commune with God. He would always go to the mountain top to commune with His Father.

Do you know that there can be something you would want to discuss with God alone which you do not want others to hear? If you do not observe a retreat, you will be like a soldier who is always fighting without taking a rest to re-plan and re-strategize. This is very dangerous. You must observe retreat to refill your spiritual cup.

8. Unbelief: This is the greatest of all prayer killers. It makes you lower the standard of the Most High. A person may shout at the loudest pitch of his voice and pray to heaven. That does not bother satan. What matters to him is what happens after the prayer and shouting. Do you believe God blindly? Are you going to take a bold step of faith or you just sit there like a gambler wanting to hit a jackpot? When a word of knowledge is released, it may be for one person, but 2,000 people can catch the overflow. That is how faith operates. In Romans 4:20-21 we read about being persuaded about God's promises. It says, "He staggered not at the promise of God through unbelief; but was strong in faith, giving glory to God. And being fully persuaded that, what he had promised, he was able also to perform."

What does it mean to be fully persuaded? It means that a person can be half-persuaded or a little bit persuaded. It is like filling a cup with water to the brim with no room to contain any extra drop. A sister had a serious trouble. Her husband came to her place of work and created a scene. He made a loud noise, as he accused his wife of being a prostitute and sleeping with the Managing Director of the company. The entire staff gathered to watch what was going on. It was really shameful and very disgraceful for the woman. Later, in the evening, when she got home, her belongings had already been thrown outside with a note of warning placed on top of them which read: "If you do not pack your luggage and go to your parents, prepare for your funeral." She packed her belongings and left and went to God in prayer. One particular day, she was in church and a word of knowledge came forth and said: "There is a woman here who has a stubborn husband. The man has divorced her but would soon return to her." The woman shouted, "Amen." The man was already in one of the far away northern states, but had got born again. One night, our Lord Jesus Christ appeared to him in his dream and caused him to begin to search for his wife whom he had earlier divorced. The day he found her, he prostrated to her and asked for forgiveness. That was how the Lord solved that problem.

Romans 4: 20-21 tells us that Abraham refused to stagger at the promise of God. A drunken man staggers and may injure himself in the process. But God stands by His words to perform them. Doubting God is behaving like a person under the influence of alcohol. You must rise up and shake yourself out of unbelief because it is a great prayer killer. You can never receive anything from God with unbelief. As powerful as prayer is, unbelief can kill it.

9. Procrastination: Some Christians always threaten to pray down heavens, but never set out at all to pray. The enemy gives them assignments that would steal their time. Some of them stay glued to the television or newspapers. They watch and read away the time they are supposed to spend for prayers. Even when God says, "Son, daughter, I want to speak to you at 9 o'clock," he or she would reply "Sorry, I need to listen to the 9 o'clock news on television." They keep pushing things forward. They make promises that they would do this or that will never do it.

10. Time wasters: Time-wasters fast a lot but do not pray. They shut man out and wouldn't let God in. The devil uses gossips, unprofitable discussions and vagabond thoughts to render them powerless. They live a planless, directionless, purposeless and disorganised prayer life. If you lack concentration or focus and live a planless life, you are a time waster and the devil will kill your prayer life.

CHAPTER THREE
THE STRATEGY OF WARFARE PRAYER

f you have carefully gone through the chapter that talks about the prayer killers, you would have noticed that none of the killers was basically called "the devil." The truth is that the devil uses any available thing in a Christian's life to kill his prayer life, for example, laziness and talkativeness. You must understand that if there were nothing spectacular about prayer, the devil would not bother about killing it. The fact is that prayer is the greatest weapon that paralyses the activities of the kingdom of darkness against mankind. Hence, the devil fights to stop it. In this sense, prayer is a battle.

PRAYER IS A BATTLE

One of the definitions of prayer is acting with God in His battle against evil. Prayer is not a preparation for battle but actually the battle itself. And once a prayer battle is going on, anything can happen in the heavenly (**Rev. 12: 7-8, 12, Psalm 2: 1-5, 9, 1 Samuel 2:10**).

There is a raging battle going on day and night between two opposing forces evoked by prayer. Whether you believe it or not, you are involved in the battle. It is going on between negative and positive powers; evil and good, the real thing and the counterfeit, light and darkness, right and wrong. We would get a clearer picture of this fact by going into the scriptures. In Daniel 10:1, Daniel saw into the spirit world. He saw something there. The Bible says he understood the vision and it propelled him into some prayers. He kept praying in verses 2, 10, 14 and 20. His prayer was heard on the first day and an angel was dispatched with the answer, but an evil angel opposed him for twenty-one days. That dark angel must have been very strong to be able to contend with an angel of light. Note that Daniel's prayer was a battle. This is what I mean when I said that prayer is a battle.

ANALYSIS OF BATTLE

As earlier mentioned, prayer is a battle between two opposing and strong kingdoms: the kingdom of light and the kingdom of darkness. As you already know, the kingdom of light constitutes God, the angels and Christians. A Christian is entitled to God' blessings, and requests for them through prayers. These blessings are brought to him by the angels whose ministry is evoked by the request made by a child of God. In other words, the angels have no work to do or errand to run when there is no prayer said anywhere. It was Daniel's prayer that provided an assignment for the angel of light as he was delegated to bring the answer to Daniel. The Bible calls them "ministering angels." They minister to God's children.

THE OPPOSING KINGDOM

This is a highly organised kingdom with various levels of authority and with its headquarters in the heavenly. This terrible kingdom is the kingdom of rebellion, wickedness and fallen angels headed by the devil called the dragon (Revelation 12: 8).

John 10:10 enumerates the primary assignment of the devil. What he does is to steal God's promises from Christians. Once he has successfully deprived them of these promises, he does not leave them empty but gives them his own "promises." This is how people become battered with satanic afflictions. Then he goes ahead to kill them both spiritually and physically. Prayer is the greatest instrument to stand against this satanic destructive assignment. This is why he would first take away the prayer life of any Christian he wants to destroy. Once that is done, all other things are easy for him.

There are millions of dark angels working with the devil. He assigns them to monitor every serious-minded Christian that constitutes a danger to his kingdom. If you notice that your prayer life is going down, know that there is a renewed satanic battle against you. So, you must stand up and start fighting. Let it be clear to you that the flesh does not want to pray. It is not interested in it, so you have to force it if you must survive.

Prayer is not the preparation for the battle; it is the battle itself. It is a serious battle where no one can be neutral. We have been born into it and we have no choice but to fight it out. We cannot run away from it. Some people got involved in it from their mother's womb and are still fighting. Some started as soon as they were born. Once your destiny has something positive to contribute to humanity, you must fight the battle. And you cannot stop the fight until the final whistle is blown. It is a life-long war. It is not a battle you can run away from any time you like. No, you are in it and a part of it. It is a fiercely contested conflict. Satan is an intelligent strategist and an obstinate fighter. He refuses to acknowledge defeat until he is completely defeated. Therefore, all the lost grounds must be recovered from him. And because he sometimes renews his attack, any ground that you have recovered from him must be properly defended. It is not enough to find yourself in the Promised Land; you must also defend it. Satan never gives up, he keeps trying. If he fails on Monday, he will come back on Tuesday. You have to consistently defend your ground.

There was a brother called Issa Jega. He was a blood drinker, whose duty was to cause accidents and drink blood and he was doing it successfully. He had three cars, including a BMW brand, but any time he wanted to operate, he would abandon all of them and take a public transport and on the way he would cause the accident, collect blood and transfer it to their spiritual blood bank. One day, he wanted to cause an accident, and as usual, went to the motor park. Immediately he entered the vehicle, and the driver wanted to move, somebody right inside cleared his throat and said: "Let us pray!" The fellow prayed a short, but powerful prayer. He covered the vehicle with the blood of Jesus, arrested blood-drinking demons, and decreed that the fire of God should surround the vehicle and that angels of God should be at the front and back of the vehicle. The vehicle moved and when it got to the spot where the man was to cause the accident, he tried but did not succeed, and they got to their destination safely. That was the first time he experienced failure. But the man did not give up. He went to the motor park in the town and took another vehicle. Unfortunately for him, the same brother who prayed in the first vehicle also boarded the same vehicle with him. As they were preparing to move again, the man cleared his throat and said, "Let us pray." The man on demonic mission then protested and said, "There is freedom of religion in this country. You have no right to impose your religion upon us. Don't pray! Don't pray!" The other passengers in the vehicle turned to him and said: "Friend, there is no cause for a fight. Let him pray, and later, you pray yours." The brother cleared his throat again and prayed as he did before. When they got to the place where the demonic man wanted to cause accident, nothing happened. So, he was determined to talk to the brother. When the brother got to the motor park, he disembarked and started moving away without knowing he had escaped accident twice. The demonic man ran after him, shouting: "Mr. Man, Mr. Man, wait." The brother waited and the demonic man asked: "Please, what is your name?" The brother told him his name. And he said, "What kind of power do you have?" The brother answered: "By the grace of God, I am a born again child of God." Then the demonic man narrated what had happened and surrendered his life to Jesus.

KEY NOTES ABOUT DANIEL'S BATTLE THROUGH PRAYER

1. His prayer broke the chains of Babylonian captivity, and Israel was free to fulfill her divine purpose.
2. It was a hot contest.
3. The invisible enemies opposed the answer to his prayer. It is these invisible forces that rule the world.
4. The visible enemies of Daniel struggled to keep him from praying.
5. Daniel chapter 10 tells us that prayer can influence the events in our lives and around us.
6. It also tells us that prayer is often a contest between angels who minister and demons that hinder.

7. It tells us that Daniel's persistent wrestle on earth while the battle raged in the heavenly was what brought the victory.
8. It tells us that prayer is heard at once in heaven but that God's messenger could be delayed on the way by the powers of darkness.
9. It tells us that sometimes if we stop praying when God's angels are on their way to bring a blessing to us, they can go back and the blessing would be lost.
10. It tells us that the fight can sometimes be very serious and even very tough for the holy angels. It means that sometimes when we are praying, delay could come because of the storms on the way of the angels coming to us with answers. There are storms in the heavenly.
11. The story of Daniel tells us that our prayer can turn the battle in our favour.
12. It tells us that satan has the power to hold the answer back for a while. He can cause delay.
13. It tells us that satan does not have the power to hold the answer back permanently. Once he is holding it and you continue to pray, he must release it eventually.
14. It tells us that praying is spiritual fighting.
15. It tells us that it is possible for one to mount a siege of prayer.
16. The story of Daniel gives us the interesting information that God's angels needed the help of Daniel to accomplish their mission.
17. It tells us that prayer is the most powerful of all the weapons God commanded us to use.
18. It tells us about the three Ps: the Promise of God, the Performance of that promise as well as Prayer. The promises of God's word are not a substitute for our prayers. They provoke our prayers. When you grab a promise and dip it into prayers, it gets to performance.
19. It tells us that it takes prayers to make the promises of God for our lives effective.

These keynotes are meant to enlighten us on the activities that take place during a prayer battle. Therefore, to make your prayer effective, you must bear these keynotes in mind and work with them.

What is likely to make the difference is if you quit. Daniel persisted and he received his desire.

WHO ARE THOSE QUALIFIED FOR THIS BATTLE?

It is possible for someone to think that he is still in the battlefield and on the winning side, while the enemy has already captured him. The devil does not bother about the prayer of some Christians because they have no effect on him and his kingdom. These Christians are called, "captured soldiers or warriors" and the type of prayer they pray is called "fireless prayer."

THE THREE CLASSES OF PEOPLE IN PRAYER BATTLE ARE:

1. Nonentities: These are people who are unserious with prayer. I call them the "rubbish class," because they are just wasting time. They are crying and the devil is rejoicing because he knows that everything they are saying has no effect on him. Unfortunately, we have many of such people in the house of God. Somebody who has just committed sin and is praying fire and militant prayers is a nonentity as far as the devil is concerned. He would wait for the person to finish the fruitless effort he calls prayer and would give him a knock on the head and that is it. He would say, "Why are you calling the name of Jesus when you are one of us? What do you mean? You belong to the nonentity class." This means that there are many prayers that never go beyond the roof of the place where they are being said.

So the "rubbish class" or nonentities talk without achieving anything. All the religious people, who are not born again, belong to this class. If you are only religious, you belong to the rubbish class. The Bible regards those who are not born again as vain people. Unfortunately, there are many people in the house of God who are not genuinely born again. If you were born again, you would not tell lies, engage in fornication, or be flirtatious. You would not steal or speak ill of others, or be proud. **Psalm 39: 5 says,** "Behold, thou hast made my days as an handbreadth; and mine age is as nothing before thee: verily every man at his best state is altogether vanity." **Psalm 62: 9:** "Surely men of low degree are vanity, and men of high degree are a lie: to be laid in the balance, they are altogether lighter than vanity."

Your membership of the church notwithstanding if you are not born again, you are praying dead prayers; prayers that do not evoke any battle in the heavenly. A sinner in a saint's robe is totally useless spiritually. As far as the devil is concerned, the lives of unbelievers do not affect him in any way, even if they pray. There are some, who can pray for hours non-stop, but they still abuse and curse their children. They are not enlisted in the prayer battle because they are not qualified for it.

2. Grasshoppers: The second class of people in prayer battle is called the grasshoppers. They go from one place to another without focus and purpose. Sometimes, they get result, but most times they don't. Just as the Israelites saw themselves as grasshoppers and said they would not be able to go to the battle against the enemies, so are the people in this class. They work by sight and see their enemies as giants. They lack the boldness and courage needed for this battle. They are not qualified because they are already captured soldiers in their own camp.

3. Giants: The third class is the giants, God's giants. These are the people who can move into the realm where they are seated with Christ in the heavenly immediately they start to pray. Such people are able to resist and overcome the enemy once they start to pray. They are bold enough to take the battle into the camp of the enemy and come out victorious. They are also called "the prayer eagles." For you to understand clearly who a prayer eagle is, I would describe his kind of prayer as follows:

a. The prayer of the prayer eagle lives longer. We know that the eagle lives longer than the average human being. The eagle lives an average of 120 years. Therefore, the prayer of the prayer eagle continues to live long after he is dead and gone to be with the Lord.

b. The prayer of the prayer eagle pursues and overtakes. We have been told that the eagle can move about 135 miles per hour. Likewise, the prayer of the prayer eagle travels at such speed to pursue and overtake.

c. His prayer can penetrate the heavenly. The eagle is called the king of all birds. By the same token, the prayer of the prayer eagle is the battle-key in the mighty conflict. The eagle is called the king of birds because of the amazing height it can ascend. It can fly over 30,000 feet above the earth, up to where airplanes cannot even get to, and where there is no gravity. Prayer can go right through the second heavens to the third heavens. No wonder, the ancient people call the eagle the bird of heaven.

d. The eagle builds its nest in the most inaccessible place on top of the rock. It is the same thing with the prayer eagles. They hide where nothing can by any means hurt them.

e. Prayer eagles see clearly. Of all creatures with feathers, the eagle has the strongest vision, the sharpest eyes. At 10,000 feet above the earth, the eagle can see a small fish inside the water. The eyes of the eagle are about eight times sharper than the eyes of man. It is also the same thing with prayer eagles. They can see what other people cannot see. They know man for what he is. They can discern and see, even though they remain quiet. For example, there is no place in the Bible where we are told to openly point out those who are witches and wizards. In fact, it is not wise to point them out. Just know them and leave them. But in your silence you can bind them.

f. Every pursuer of prayer eagles never succeeds. The eagle can discern its prey from afar off. When it is high up in the air and men cannot even see it, it can see everybody. Not only this, the eagle is the only bird that can look directly at the sun and fly towards it. So, when an enemy is pursuing the eagle, it simply locates the direction of the scotching sun, and fly towards it and the pursuer cannot get half way with it because of the heat and rays of sun.

g. Prayer eagles have power and courage. The eagle is a powerful and courageous bird. It can seize a big animal five times above its own size and carry it away with its claws. Prayer too has nothing to do with your size.

h. Prayer eagles' lives are renewed. The eagle also renews its youth. Sometimes when its feathers are old and ugly, it sheds them off and puts on new and beautiful ones. That is why prayer eagles look younger than their age. If you see a person who is a prayer eagle, he looks a lot younger than his age. They reform their vigour even at old age.

i. Prayer eagles feed on the blood of the enemy (Numbers 23: 24). Eagles feed on flesh and blood, they do not eat rubbish.

j. Prayer eagles are burden bearers and intercessors. They are fresh and energetic. Not only that, the training school of the eagle is very tough, likewise the school of prayer eagles. The eagle trains its young to fly. It throws them out, and when they are about to hit the ground it catches them. It trains its young to be able to look at the sun. Any baby eagle that is not able to look straight at the sun is killed by the mother-eagle. Prayer the enemy cannot pursue eagles.

Many people realise that they have battles to fight but discover that they lack the power to pray. When you become a prayer eagle, you will be the first to launch the attack. You do not wait for the devil to take control before you overthrow him. You pray preventive and attacking prayers. You do not have to wait until your whole business is messed up before you start pleading the blood of Jesus upon it. Prayer eagles don't beg the devil to leave them alone, they order him to leave and not come near them again.

A brother once told me that whenever a certain man in his place of work arrived at the office every morning, he would close his eyes and pray for fifteen minutes before he commenced work. He did the same thing in the evenings before leaving the office. He was the only one who would not crack jokes in the staff bus on their way home; he would only be praying. After just one month in a particular unit, the man was promoted. And shortly after that he was promoted again and transferred to another unit. That is what happens to those who can pray.

Actually, anyone who can pray does not have any problem. A person would have problem only if he cannot pray. Prayer eagles fight the battle at the enemy's gate. They do not allow it to take place at their own gate. They pray about what they cannot see, and cause trouble where they have not even stepped their feet. These are the kinds of things that the Lord wants us to be doing. Prayer eagles are also called "prayer warriors." Let us know who they are.

CHARACTERISTICS OF PRAYER WARRIORS

1. They grow spiritually. They are not stagnant or slow in spiritual growth. The Bible says we should desire the sincere milk of the word of God so that we can grow. There are rules that guide the growth of a normal child likewise a Christian that desires spiritual growth.

Rules governing the growth of a Christian:
Daily intake of food: The daily food of the Christian is the word of God. Regular reading, studying and meditating on the word of God is very necessary. Do not read just to calm your spirit. There are many materials on guidelines for Bible reading and memorisation of scriptures. Bible reading and study should not be done hurriedly. You should absorb the word of God.

- **Oxygen:** The Christian should also always take spiritual oxygen, which makes the soul grow.
- **Exercise:** This represents your service unto the Lord. For example, witnessing gives you the chance of exercising yourself. Just make sure you are doing something for God.
- **Rest:** This represents your absolute trust in God for all things. Rely on God at all times.
- **Cleanliness:** You need to keep good company and maintain a clean spiritual environment. Avoid friends that would hinder your growth and environment that can corrupt your mind. Evil communication corrupts good manners. If you live your life as

God expects, some unbelievers will avoid you because they will find you difficult to cope with. An unbeliever must not feel comfortable with a born again Christian. If they come to your house expecting to be entertained with alcoholic drinks and you serve them soft drinks, they will not be happy.

Care: Do not forsake the assembly of the children of God. Attend fellowship meetings and be your brother's keeper.

Periodic check-up: Examine yourself from time to time and confess all known and unknown sins as enjoined by 1 Corinthians 11:31.

2. They are dead to self: Let God pull self out of you. That is, things that are not of God must be put to death in your life. Anybody who means business with God must go to the spiritual graveyard and bury the flesh.

A young boy wanted to give the totality of his life to God and was becoming very serious. And God told him that if he wanted Him to use him, He would first of all kill him. The boy did not understand that God was referring to the flesh in him. One day, as he was praying, he heard his friends downstairs playing football. A voice told him to stop praying and join them. Another voice told him to continue praying. The battle went on until God said, "That was the flesh. That is why it must die." He then got up and commanded the evil voice telling him to join his friends to keep quiet, and continued praying. About six months later, he moved into his room to pray and as soon as he opened his mouth, he felt the presence of God and saw His glory. He fell flat on his face and God took him in a vision to heaven. Later, God showed him the vision of how angels buried his flesh. From then on, flesh had no more dominion over his life.

This is the hardest thing for Christians to do. Some people wonder why some Christians come to church and hear sermons, but the sermons have no effect on their lives. It is because the flesh is the ruler of their lives. The hardest thing for a Christian to do is to bring his desire, ambition and habit right to the feet of the cross and leave them there; and become like Paul who said, "I am crucified with Christ, nevertheless I live but the life which I now live, I live in Christ who is in me." The old Paul was dead and the new one was alive. No wonder those demons said to the sons of Sceva, "Paul, we know, Jesus, we know, who are you?" The flesh was still alive in them so they could not make any impact to the kingdom of darkness. One secret that many people do not know is that the most exciting and beautiful spiritual life will not start until flesh or self dies. It is then you can walk by the Spirit. Then God can open your spiritual as you are walking in the street and show you things that the ordinary eyes cannot see. You would see that the people walking in the street are not the way the ordinary eyes are seeing them. You would see that some are carrying coffins on their heads and some are carrying dirty pillowcases.

When flesh dies, your spirit eyes will open. Things that you used to see as coincidences will no longer be so to you. You will understand how God moves. Until you die to self, God cannot use you the way He wants. You cannot die partially or be half-alive unto God. You must get to the point where you are completely emptied of self and only God will be in you. Unless you die to the flesh, you would continue to be ridiculed spiritually even if you were performing miracles. The devil can still mess you up because the flesh is still alive in you. When someone who is dead to the flesh begins to pray, things will happen fast according to the promise in Isaiah, which says: "While they are yet speaking, I will answer them."

3. They have uncompromising faith: God acted for Shadrach, Meschack and Abednego the way He did because they refused to compromise their faith. Many people misquote the Bible. They would say: "Give unto Caesar what is Caesar's." Therefore, when they are dealing with unbelievers, they behave like them. They also use it as an excuse to push the scriptures aside when it is not convenient for them. The truth is that they are not Caesar's image but God's and God wants them to give themselves to Him.

When you don't compromise your faith, God gets excited about you and can depend on you wherever you are. For example, if God is looking for a believer, who will minister life to people at his or her place of work, and sees that Sister A spends hours making up, Sister B gets angry easily, Brother C is always combing his moustache, and Brother D drinks wine secretly and claims not to be drinking alcohol. It means that all of them have failed God and the blood of their colleagues who did not hear the gospel would be required from them. The three Hebrew boys maintained their stand in God. When you compromise with evil as a believer, God will not come to you when you get into trouble. That is why Jesus said, "Whosoever is ashamed of me in this adulterous generation, of him will I be ashamed in the kingdom of my Father."

A Christian should not compromise. You can't stay in Egypt and confess that you are in the Promised Land. You can't glue yourself to the world and say that you don't want to be a fanatic. Jesus was a fanatic and said all He wanted to say dogmatically. If you leave your children to do what they like, for example, watch pornographic films or stay at home while you come to church, you are compromising. When a believer gets involved in shady business, he is compromising his faith. A believer who compromises his faith cannot be prayer warrior or a giant in the battlefield.

As you pay attention to these rules, your growth is sure. If not, you will be stagnant.

WHAT IS WARFARE PRAYER?

Warfare prayer is the kind of prayer that brings the victory of Jesus over the host of evil. The Bible refers to believers as soldiers. You don't join the armed forces with the promise that you would not shoot anybody and nobody would shoot you, or that you would not see blood at all. That is not how your spirit would operate. We are to uphold the victory of Jesus over the host of evil. The victory Jesus won can be summed up in the following words: "All authority in heaven and on earth has been given unto me and at the name of Jesus, every knee should bow." When you uphold all authority against evil, you are praying warfare prayer.

Warfare prayer is a prayer to hinder evil operation in a life, place, or thing. Just as Moses' hands were held up until victory was won, so the prayer warrior holds up the victory of Christ over evil until his victory is won.

Warfare prayers are prayers directed at the host of hell. Mountain of Fire and Miracles Ministries does not pray against any physical person. We pray against the host of hell. If anybody decides to form a covenant with the host of hell and to issue a curse against the child of God, whatever happens to the host of hell can happen to the person. And nobody can blame the believer for that. If the believer says the spirit of witchcraft should fall down and die and somebody somewhere says, "No, instead of me to leave the spirit of witchcraft, I would rather die with it," so be it.

Christians have been praying all kinds of prayers since the beginning of Christianity. Certain prayers do not bother the devil at all, but there are some that really worry him. One of such prayers is "warfare prayer."

HOW TO PRAY WARFARE PRAYER

1. **Declare your faith:** You start by making some scriptural confessions. Then you go on to praise and worship. Bold declaration of your faith is warfare praying. Somebody, who stands up and says, "Through the blood of Jesus, I am justified, through the blood of Jesus I have peace," is praying warfare prayer.

2. **Resist the devil:** When you say, resist, it means that you do not want to give that thing any chance. There is a Bible passage that says, "Be angry, but sin not, let not the sun set on your anger." Another verse says, "Give the enemy no place," meaning that your anger can create a place for the enemy. So, if you want to resist the devil, when he says, "Okay begin to boil with anger," you would say, "No, I refuse to boil, in Jesus' name."

3. **Confess your sins:** Confess your sins to the Lord. Tell Him that you are sorry for your sins. Don't ever see yourself as pure or sinless when approaching God's throne in prayer. Confess both

known and unknown sins. This is very serious because it is sin that will give the devil a foothold. Once you confess it to the Lord, the devil will have nowhere to hide in your life. That way, he will lose the first stage of the battle.

4. **Forgive those who have sinned against you:** If anybody has offended you, forgive him or her and ask the Lord to forgive you for not forgiving the person before that time. If you don't forgive the person, you will start losing the battle before it begins because you would be released into the hands of what the Bible calls tormentors and they will torment you day and night.

5. **Use the blood of Jesus:** Cover yourself and everyone connected with you with the blood of Jesus. Also cover your environment with the blood. The power in the blood of Jesus during warfare is wonderful.

6. **Break soul-ties:** This is compulsory for anyone who has ever indulged in premarital or extramarital sex, or anyone who has been involved in rituals as dictated by satanic priests and fake prophets. Such a person's life would remain under the control of the demons that monitor such evil acts and warfare prayer is needed to break them. A certain man got married on a Saturday and the following Sunday, he rushed back with a complaint that he was not settled as he could not keep his mind off his former girl friend who had equally married. That is the effect of evil soul-tie covenant.

7. **Command release from evil domination and control:** When a person says: "I refuse evil to dominate me" or "I refuse evil to control me," he is praying a great warfare prayer. Release from evil domination is necessary for spiritual growth.

8. **Command release from acquired and inherited bondage:** When a person has acquired or inherited bondage, the kind of prayer that would set him or her free is warfare prayer.

9. **Break curses, charms, jinxes and bewitchment:** When you break a curse or a spell, or command a charm to become powerless, or decree that a jinx should not continue to operate, or release something from bewitchment, you are praying warfare prayer.

10. **Renounce your membership of the occult:** When somebody who was a member of a secret society or a wrong church where they practice unscriptural things pulls out of the place and is renouncing his involvement there, it is warfare praying.
11. **Destroy evil communication:** When you pray that you do not want anything evil to communicate with you, you are praying warfare prayer.
12. **Take authority over the strongman wherever he may be.**
13. **Command satan to release all he has stolen from you:** For you to claim back everything the enemy has stolen from you, you can say: "Satan, I want all you have stolen from me back sevenfold now, in the name of Jesus." It is warfare prayer.
14. **Arrest and bind territorial spirits:** There must be some spirits that control the territory where you live. You arrest them and bind their powers. There is nowhere in the world that is free. Anywhere you find yourself, do warfare praying. If a believer happens to travel out and has to lodge in a hotel, he must arrest every spirit there because he never can tell the kind of person that slept on that bed before him.
15. **Claim back lost ground:** A lost ground can be claimed back through warfare praying.
16. **Praises:** Praise the Lord always. The enemies of our soul can attack many areas of our lives. They can attack the physical body through diseases, food and physical objects. These things require warfare praying. When an object is made for occult purposes, it would carry some powers. If a person touches the thing or hangs it on his neck, the demons attached to it would enter his body. The only way to get them out is warfare prayer.

It would be 100 per cent foolishness for a man to assume that since he grew up in a Christian home and his parents are Christians, he does not need deliverance, and therefore does not need to pray aggressively. Some men of God in England spent two days praying for a girl of 17 who had never visited Nigeria, to deliver her from evil spirits. She was born in England and had been there all her life. She had never travelled to Nigeria. But to their shock, demons from Nigeria began to cry out of her body.

The truth is that millions of apparently normal and respectable people need serious deliverance. Many have gone to several places for protection. But if you say, "Well, we do praise worship and there is no problem." You should know that praise worship that is done from unclean lips does not go anywhere. The devil can do most of the things we do in the house of God a lot better. The only thing he cannot do is prayer. It is not a joke that the largest church in the world is the church where prayer takes 90 per cent of the time and every other thing takes 10 per cent.

What the church of God needs now is a surgeon and not a cosmetologist. We must go back to traditional Pentecostal hard praying. Then we would throw fear into the camp of the enemies again and they will know without being told that no matter how far they have travelled, there is a power that can catch up with them in just one second and disgrace them.

CHAPTER FOUR
SPIRITUAL WARFARE BY REVELATION

Our God is a warrior. David knew this great attribute of God and declared in **Psalm 144: 1:** "Blessed be the Lord my strength, which teacheth my hands to war, and my fingers to fight."

This section of this book is loaded with more facts for Christians in the school of spiritual warfare and all those who want to be consistently victorious over the enemy in all battles of life.

Knowledge, wisdom, revelation and information are very interesting words in the Bible. The word "information" refers to the collection of data, which gives knowledge. Knowledge is the possession of information. Wisdom, on the other hand, is the ability to apply knowledge. Only only the Almighty God gives Revelation. There are many professors and doctors whose lives are in a total mess. They have information, wisdom and knowledge but have no revelation because they do not belong to God and so cannot hear from Him.

2 Kings 6: 8-12 says, "Then the king of Syria warred against Israel, and took counsel with his servants, saying, In such and such a place shall be my camp. And the man of God sent unto the king of Israel, saying, Beware that thou pass not such a place; for thither the Syrians are come down. And the king of Israel sent to the place, which the man of God told him and warned him of, and saved himself there, not once nor twice. Therefore the heart of the king of Syria was sore troubled for this thing; and he called his servants, and said unto them, Will ye not shew me which of us is for the king of Israel? And one of his servants said, None, my lord, O king: but Elisha, the prophet that is in Israel, telleth the king of Israel the words that thou speakest in thy bedchamber."

If the man of God had not told the king of Israel where the enemy was coming from, the king and his servants would have fallen into the hands of the enemy and the enemy would have rounded them up and finished them. The Syrian king was worried that all his plans were foiled and he wanted to know if any of his servants was a spy. He was told that it was Elisha, the man of God, who could hear what he the king was discussing in his bedchamber thousands of kilometres away, and was revealing them to the king of Israel. I pray that the Lord will promote you to that level, in the name of Jesus.

It is possible to get to the level where you can hear witches and wizards discussing and right there you can scatter them. Sometimes, they come to Christian gatherings and would be talking and laying out strategies for catching the children of God. You cannot hear them with ordinary ears, until God opens your spiritual ears. The power that enables you to know such things is revelation power. Also, if you want breakthroughs, you must learn how to move by revelation, not by knowledge, information or wisdom. All these are human intellect. Move by revelation.

Verses 13-16 say, "Here, the king of Syria asked his servants to spy out Elisha and they told him he was in Dothan. Today, many powers are spying on the children of God, watching for their unguarded hour to make them sin against God, or to destroy them. I pray that such evil monitoring eyes spying on you shall be plucked out, in the name of Jesus. The king of Syria mobilised a whole army against one person: but Elisha, being a man of God and having revelation knowledge, saw them and knew that the host of heaven was with him, so he did not panic. His servant did not see the host of heaven with them and so, he was afraid. Elisha had to pray for him, that God should open his eyes so that he would see. Many Christians today are spiritually blind, like Elisha's servant. Verses 17-18: "And Elisha prayed, and said, Lord, I pray thee, open his eyes, that he may see. And the Lord opened the eyes of the young man; and he saw: and, behold, the mountain was full of horses and chariots of fire round about Elisha. And when they came down to him, Elisha prayed unto the Lord, and said, Smite this people, I pray thee, with blindness. And he smote them with blindness according to the word of Elisha."

When I was in England, an elder in our church told us how revival broke out in the church many years back. He said there was a brother who always saw one revelation or the other each time they prayed. So, after every prayer meeting, they would ask him what he saw. One day, he said he saw three demons sitting on the wall of the church and they refused to leave despite all the prayers. The prayer warriors decided to come back at night to pray and chase those demons away. They came as arranged and as they were praying, the demons fell one after the other and never came back. Shortly after that, revival broke out in the church and many people gave their lives to the Lord Jesus Christ. The ability to hear and see beyond the physical realms is a great asset in spiritual warfare.

One day, a sister came for prayer but hurried away because the man of God did not attend to her on time. She nagged and left, saying she was going to fight the strange woman who was occupying the attention of her husband when she got to the strange woman she undressed and this sister did not know that she should flee. Underneath the strange woman were charms and the sister said it was disgusting that her husband could move with women like that. Instead of leaving, the sister waited until the woman brought out a calabash, and from inside it she heard the voice of her own mother, ordering the strange woman to deal ruthlessly with the sister. She could not believe her ears but that was how trouble started and all sorts of things happened to her which eventually led to her death.

If that sister was able to hear and see spiritually, she would have known the kind of person the woman was and she would have dismantled those strange powers right from her own sitting room through warfare prayer.

A very old man of God told me that when he got born again, he was very hot for the Lord. He was a preacher in a village. At that time, there was an epidemic of small pox in all the surrounding villages. One night, the Lord told him that the demon of small pox was going to bring small pox at 3. a.m. and that he should go to the entrance of the village at 3.a.m. and deal with the demon in the name of Jesus. This man of

God told me that he went and found the dwarf creature with a calabash and he dealt with it in the name of Jesus and the demon left. That village never had the out-break of small pox and nobody knew why.

As a young Christian, I was ignorant of certain things. One day, a sister was rolling on the floor, holding her belly. We started praying and binding the spirit of stomach ache. After some time, one of us who was more sensitive to spiritual things said we should stop praying and ask her what she had done. The sister confessed that she had just gone through an abortion. This was at the moment she was about to breathe her last. The power of revelation was able to enlighten our ignorance.

The bat is a blind animal and there are many spiritual bats in the church today. The trouble with the spiritual life of a prayer bat is that the person would be frustrated in the end because he would not be able to move by revelation. Most of the attacks that Christians go through have spiritual background and origin. Many people are ignorant of this fact, hence they lose woefully. They live their lives in defeat, frustration and confusion. I pray that this will not be your portion, in the name of Jesus.

In a spiritual battle, there are two sides: actors and reactors. Actors are those who see the plans and purposes of the enemy and take immediate steps to avert danger and calamity. Reactors are those who start fighting after the enemy has struck. The Lord has given every believer the Holy Spirit so that they can see things to come and then do spiritual warfare about them. Some of the dreams that people have that are very scary are actually future plans and purposes of the enemy. God reveals them so that they can pray about them and cancel them.

Some prophets get confused at this stage. They see the plan of the enemy and become scared, but the enemy does not have the last say. Sometimes, when God Himself has decided to do something, either to correct or punish, if someone stands in the gap and intercedes, he can avert such a thing and God would change His mind. Jonah knew that God would forgive the people of Nineveh and so, did not want to go and preach to them.

I am always challenged by the fact that God could show a vision to an unbeliever about things that would happen to the world. This has happened right from the time of Babylon. It happens in this present day and will continue to happen even unto the end of the world. Thousands of years ago, God showed Nebuchadnezzar certain events that would happen in the world. Many of those things have happened, many are still happening and the rest will still happen. Hence, Christians should occupy their space in the revelation world, so that they can tap from the very heart of God.

THE ROLE OF THE HOLY SPIRIT IN REVELATION WARFARE

John 16:13: "Howbeit when he, the Spirit of truth, is come, he will guide you into all truth: for he shall not speak of himself; but whatsoever he shall hear, that shall he speak: and he will shew you things to come."

If you understand this message and put it to use, any herbalist or witch that works against you simply wants to bury himself or herself because even before he or she starts, you would have seen his or her plans and would have scattered everything.

John 16:4: "But these things have I told you, that when the time shall come, ye may remember that I told you of them. And these things I said not unto you at the beginning, because I was with you."

1 Corinthians 2:9: "But as it is written, Eye hath not seen, nor ear heard, neither have entered into the heart of man, the things which God hath prepared for them that love him."

This passage shows us that no spirit can know the secret of a person more than his own spirit. So also, no other spirit knows the secret of God more than the Spirit of God. The Holy Spirit can reveal deep and secret things to you and can search out all things. The trouble, however, is that many people are impatient and many know too much. Many claim to have brain knowledge but not spiritual knowledge.

1 Corinthians 12:7-11: "But the manifestation of the Spirit is given to every man to profit withal. For to one is given by the Spirit the word of wisdom; to another the word of knowledge by the same Spirit; To another faith by the same Spirit; to another the gifts of healing by the same Spirit; To another the working of miracles; to another prophecy; to another discerning of spirits; to another divers kinds of tongues; to another the interpretation of tongues: But all these worketh that one and the selfsame Spirit, dividing to every man severally as he will."

Apart from being the comforter, the Holy Spirit holds the office of the Teacher, Energizer, Intercessor and Revealer. He spies for the Almighty God. You could be praying and suddenly find yourself at a meeting where you are the subject of discussion. The Holy Spirit would tell you to listen attentively. To your surprise, the following morning, physically, you see one of the people whose faces you saw at the witchcraft meeting. The person brings food to you and the Holy Spirit says you should be calm, take the food but do not eat it. This is one of the ways the Lord reveals things that witches plan against God's children.

From the passages above you can see that the Holy Spirit guides, hears, speaks and shows things to come. He knows the things of God and of the devil and reveals them to the children of God. He knows deep and secret things by God, searches out all things and makes us know them freely as given to us by God. The reason the white garment false prophets have succeeded in confusing many people is that they claim to see visions. Unfortunately, many intellectuals, who are spiritual bats, have lost their property and even their wives to these people. In order to have a proper functioning of the Holy Spirit in us as the Revealer, we must reverence Him because He is a personality. God does not like being used, so you must approach Him with thanksgiving in your heart and with praises. When you want the Holy Spirit to descend, you do not just go ahead and ask Him to do this and that, you must enter His gates with thanksgiving in your heart and into His courts with praise. You must develop an intimate, dynamic relationship with Him.

HOW TO DEVELOP A SWEET COMMUNION WITH THE HOLY SPIRIT

- Acknowledge Him daily.
- Praise Him daily.

- Listen to Him daily.
- Obey Him daily.
- Worship Him daily.
- Talk to Him daily.

MECHANISMS OF SPIRITUAL REVELATION

The will of God for us is that even before the enemy attacks we must have had fore-knowledge of it. We should have known who wants to attack, how and the nature of the attack, the weapons he wants to employ and ways of counteracting him. Job is a very interesting book of the Bible. One day, the host of hell decided to deal with Job and, one day, the physical manifestation took place. If you have spiritual revelation of the moment the host of hell decides to take on you, you would counter it before the set day for the physical manifestation. You may have to fast and pray. Sometimes, a revelation is positive, so you will have to pray and fast that it will happen safely.

I was invited to a meeting one day and as we were praying, the Lord showed me a wedding dress stained with blood. I asked the newly-wedded couples and those intending to get married to come out and they did. Then we prayed. The following Saturday, a newly-wedded couple was coming back from the reception hall and their vehicle went off the road and almost dropped into the lagoon. The railing of the bridge held it back. Rescuers had to hold the vehicle and carry it off the railing for the couple to come down. The bride's dress was stained with blood, but thank God, no one died. This couple was one of those who came out on that day for prayers. The devil did not kill them because the situation had been spiritually addressed.

The Spirit of God, by revelation, enabled Elisha to hear and see the secrets of the enemies of Israel and he was enable to pass spiritual intelligence report to the king. The prophets in a church are the intelligence team of that church. The information received by Elisha helped Israel not to fall into the snare of the enemies. It also enabled Elisha to be bold and confident and to capture his enemies alive. We need to pray that God should open our spiritual eyes so that we can see, and our spiritual ears so that we can hear the things that the Spirit of God is trying to show and tell us.

1 Corinthians 12 shows us the need for spiritual gifts. This is an area where many Christians have neglected, especially those in business. The Bible says we should desire the spiritual gift of revelation. This is the gift that makes us know things supernaturally. If you want to become a millionaire or a billionaire, pray to receive these gifts. For example, with the word of knowledge, Elisha was able to detect Gehazi. He said his eyes went with him as he went to meet Naaman. It was the gift that made him locate the Syrian army. This gift made Paul to know that the journey on the ship would be hazardous to both lives and property. He told the ship crew but they disregarded him until it happened.

With the gift of wisdom, Jesus was able to deal with the people who accused a woman of adultery. They caught the woman in the very act of adultery but they brought only the woman and left the man. They claimed that the law of Moses condemned her to death. He did not say a word, He bent down and wrote on the sand. The Bible does not tell us what He wrote but He could have written things that reminded the accusers themselves of their own sins.

With the gift of discernment, Paul was able to detect that the girl hailing him and Silas had a familiar spirit. She said the right thing but was fake and Paul knew it. Through this gift, you will know what is going on in a given situation and you will take action. One day, a man wearing white agbada, drove to the front of my house in a Mercedes Benz V-Boot Car, got off the car and started rolling on the ground, saying he was dead. I was called and I moved close and asked him what the matter was. He said he invested in a business and was duped. He had supplied the goods with a loan he got to do the job. When he went to collect his money, he found that the office was empty. He was in great debt. He ran to the police station and they discovered that all the documents he was given were fake. If the man had the gift of discerning of spirits, he would have known that those people were not to be trusted and he wouldn't have had any business deal with them.

If you start going into the word of God and allow the Holy Spirit to take control of your life, you will receive the gift of the Spirit. If you have the gift of revelation, the gift of speaking in diverse tongues and interpretation of tongue and the gift of prophecy, God can talk to you through them. These gifts of the Spirit are not for pastors alone. They are for everybody, no matter what your vocation is, once you surrender your life to the Lord Jesus Christ, you can receive them. You should pray to have these gifts. You must submit your totality to the Lord as a living sacrifice and must be completely broken. When the gift of the word of knowledge is operating in your life, you can tell the condition or whereabouts of a particular thing, even when it is not possible to know it naturally and when you do not pray about it specifically.

Although the purpose of these gifts is to find lost souls and to populate heaven, it also helps to find lost articles and to get useful information. God can make you know where the right customers are. God can make you know the character and nature of the customer. God is concerned about every detail about our lives and can show you areas of profitable operation either in your dream or vision or through audible voice. When you receive such supernatural revelation, you will know better how to pray.

You have to stop gambling with your life. Find out what God wants you to do and go ahead and do it. Do not experiment. Until you are sure of what God wants you to do, don't commit your money or life to anything. If you do, you are likely to lose. Through the word of wisdom, God will show you how, why, when, where and the worth of a matter. Whatever vocation you are involved in, you need this gift. Every businessman should have it. Every student, preacher, teacher, etc needs it everyday.

KEYS TO MOVING IN REVELATION KNOWLEDGE

1. Be dissatisfied with your present state and seek improvement in your spiritual level. The first key to the healing of blind Bartimaeus was that he was dissatisfied with his state. There is no reason unbelievers should become multi-millionaires and the

children of God are poor when the Holy Spirit is there to help them in any situation. It is the children of God that can get baptised in the Holy Ghost and have spiritual gifts.

2. Be determined. You have to make up your mind to make moves that will bring about improvement in your spiritual life. A lot of people are not satisfied with their state but they are not mad about a change yet. They are not determined to have a change.

3. Become desperate. Once a person gets to the level of desperation, progress starts and his eyes open.

With these three facts you can get into your desired level of spiritual experience.

BECOMING GOD'S SPY

You must be born again and come to the saving knowledge of the Lord Jesus Christ before you can belong to Him. Thereafter; you have to die to self so that He can take preeminence in your life. Then stay away from demonic pollution.

STRATEGIES FOR BECOMING GOD'S SPY

1. Learn to be alone with God in a quiet place so that He can give you directives and you will hear Him clearly. Elijah heard the still small voice of God and was able to summon up courage.
2. Shut out distractions, that is, anything that can divert your attention. Some people kneel down to pray and suddenly remember that there is something boiling on fire or that there are cloths on the line outside or that something has been plugged into electricity and must be disconnected. All these make the person lose concentration.
3. Ask the Lord one question at a time and wait for an answer.
4. Pray with expectation and know that as you pray, God will answer you.

5. Remove your emotion from what you are praying about. If you are emotionally attached to any part of the answers, negative or positive, you may not receive an answer. For example, a sister who already accepts lifts and gifts from a brother and has started going to his house, now prays, asking God if the brother is His will for her would not hear any thing from God, because she has already made her choice. It is like a cheque, which has the amount filled in, signed and given to a messenger to deliver. God does not deliver evil messages.
6. Note that God is not talkative. He says something and it stands.
7. Learn to wait patiently before God and listen to Him. Prayer is always a two-way conversation. If your prayer is just one way: you talk and ask and do not want to hear from God, you will not make a headway.

There is quantity prayer and there is quality prayer. Quantity prayer is long and goes on for a long time without having substance. Quality prayer could be long or short but has substance. Christians cheat themselves a lot by not waiting to hear from God. If you listen, the Holy Spirit will talk to you about everything and anything. When you begin to practise this, it becomes a habit and you will not take any step without asking the Holy Spirit to guide you. Sometimes, the Holy Spirit answers back by showing you a picture or an object. The normal thing for a person who wants to hear from God and learn is to ask Him what that means. This kind of exercise is not for those who are in a hurry. They are for those who are patient before the Lord and want God to talk to them.

The reason most people cannot hear from God is that their minds are full of their own opinions and thoughts, which can be a barrier to God's intention and communication with them. Anyone who wants information from the Lord must look at every situation without bias, without speculation or suspicion. Once you start, it becomes a habit.
8. Learn how to stay free of pollution. God will not pour His gifts into an unholy vessel. God will not talk to you if you are polluted within or without.

HOW TO STAY FREE FROM POLLUTION

a. Read your Bible daily. Both faith and belief come from what you read. Study the word of God, meditate on it and memorise Scriptures because what is in your heart will eventually come out of your mouth.

b. Pray every day. Deliberately yield yourself every morning to prayers.

c. Learn to plead the blood of Jesus over yourself, family, work, school and possession.

d. Put on the whole armour of God as written in Ephesians 6:10-17.

e. Stay filled with the Holy Spirit: speak in tongues. When your life is filled with the Holy Spirit, it is difficult to get other materials inside.

f. Avoid all situations that cause or encourage sin. It could be things, places or people. If going to a place makes you fall into sin, don't go there anymore.

g. Stop worrying and getting anxious. Do not allow worry and anxiety to come into your mind. Once your heart is troubled, God cannot speak to you.

h. Resist the devil and he will flee. Tell him to pack his luggage and flee.

i. Pay your tithes and offerings regularly so that God will drive away devourers from your finances. Devourers are demons that can come in if you fail to pay your tithes and offerings.

j. Praise the Lord in all things.

As the years are rolling in and out, people lose a lot of things due to lack of revelation. I want you to examine your life and see what lack of revelation has caused in your life. Those who have revelation knowledge would be laughing while others are crying because they cannot go to the courtroom of heaven and see the decision taken concerning their situation. Spiritual blindness leads to frustration because the Lord might have finished preparing and perfecting everything you want Him to do and has set a table before you in the presence of your enemies, but because you are weary with worry, sick and blind spiritually, you are likely to use your legs to knock down the table that God has set before you. Those that can see spiritually are human beings like you. So, cry unto the Lord to open your eyes and ears today.

CHAPTER FIVE
WHEN PRAYERS BECOME SIN

We shall start this section by looking at four strange scriptures:

Psalm 109:7: "And he led them forth by the right way, that they might go to a city of habitation." This means that it is possible for prayer to become sin.

Psalm 80:4: "O Lord God of hosts, how long wilt thou be angry against the prayer of thy people?" God was not angry because they prayed. He was angry because of the kind of prayer they prayed. It is possible that God gets angry because you are praying, while if you had kept quiet, nothing would have happened. These are very strange things.

Psalm 35:13: "But as for me, when they were sick, my clothing was sackcloth: I humbled my soul with fasting; and my prayer returned into mine own bosom." This simply means that prayer can backfire. It can bounce back at the person that prayed it.

Proverb 28:9: "If a wise man contendeth with a foolish man, whether he rage or laugh, there is no rest."

Someone gave an example of what abomination could mean. He said armed robbers entered into a house and saw a pregnant woman. They asked her to bring her money and she said she had nothing. They took a knife and cut her tummy open and brought out the foetus of the twins she was carrying in her womb. Of course, she died as the pregnancy was destroyed. This is an example of an abomination. Your reaction to this incident, the way you must have shuddered, is the way God feels when prayers become an abomination.

MFM is a praying ministry. The Bible says, "My house shall be a house of prayer unto all nations." But there are some situations when prayers can become sin. It is a fearful fact but it is true that not all prayers are good. Wrong praying or what the Bible calls praying amiss is as sinful as not praying at all.

PRAYING AMISS

There is something the Bible calls praying amiss. Let me give you an example:

In 1994, a sister came to a brother and asked him to pray with her for a new job. She was leading the prayer and suddenly she began to prophesy: "Thus says the Lord, this sister whose hands you are holding as you pray, is your wife. Do you hear what the Lord is saying? She is your wife." This was a sinful prayer. Any prayer meeting that anybody summons to pray against a particular person is witchcraft prayer. The Mountain of Fire and Miracles Ministries do not pray against human beings. What we pray against are spiritual entities. One of the most serious prayers in the Bible is found in the book of Psalms, but the Psalmist was addressing his spiritual enemies. When he had the opportunity to kill Saul, he said, "God forbid that I would kill God's anointed." So, he took Saul's spear and water bottle to show him later that he really had the opportunity of killing him. He now stood afar and called the king to tell him that his guards were not doing their job well, that if he wanted he would have slain him.

Prayer to abort pregnancy, which resulted from fornication, is sinful. When you owe a person and you are praying for him to forget the money, so that you will not pay him back, it is sinful. Prayer on evil concoction or alcohol before drinking it is sinful, because in the first instance you are not supposed to take them. Prayer to extort money from others or snatch a person's wife or husband, or that the spouse of a person should die so that you would marry him or her, is sinful. Prayer to divorce your husband or wife is sinful. Job's wife told him to curse God and die. This was a sinful prayer hence, Job refused to comply.

The act of biblical praying is gradually getting lost. The act of reading the Bible to know what to pray is phasing out gradually. The Almighty is not pleased with the prayers of nowadays. Many people need to repent and reorganise their prayer lives; so that they would not be praying amiss. God is not happy with someone who is misusing the greatest source of power on earth as if it was a powerful fetish.

Prayer could be sinful; it could annoy God or become an abomination. What a sad thing that when a person phones heaven, it rings, the receiver is picked up, the caller introduces himself and the reaction is that it is slammed on the caller's ear with heaven saying: "Unclean words are not welcome. No pollution wanted!"

SINFUL PRAYERS
1. Praying with an idol in the heart: Ezekiel 9:1-3 says, "He cried also in mine ears with a loud voice, saying, Cause them that have charge over the city to draw near, even every man with his destroying weapon in his hand. And, behold, six men came from the way of the higher gate, which lieth toward the north, and every man a slaughter weapon in his hand; and one man among them was clothed with linen, with a writer's inkhorn by his side: and they went in, and stood beside the brasen altar. And the glory of the God of Israel was gone up from the cherub, whereupon he was, to the threshold of the house. And he called to the man clothed with linen, which had the writer's inkhorn by his side." **Verse 6:** "Slay utterly old and young, both maids, and little children, and women: but come not near any man upon whom is the mark; and begin at my sanctuary. Then they began at the ancient men, which were before the house." **Verse 8:** "And it came to pass, while they were slaying them, and I was left, that I fell upon my face, and cried, and said, Ah Lord God! wilt thou destroy all the residue of Israel in thy pouring out of thy fury upon Jerusalem?"

Ezekiel was praying with an idol in his heart. God was already offended by the people. They refused to listen to His commandment. Ezekiel prayed: "Please, don't destroy them, will you finish everybody?" While Ezekiel was still praying, look at what happened in verse 11: "And, behold, the man clothed with linen, which had the inkhorn by his side, reported the matter, saying, I have done as thou hast commanded me." It means that the answer to his prayer was "No."

Ezekiel 14: 3-4 says: "Son of man these men have set up their idols in their heart, and put the stumbling block of their iniquity before their face: should I be enquired of at all by them? Therefore speak unto them and say unto them, Thus saith the Lord God. Every man from the house of Israel that setteth up his idols in his heart, and putteth the stumbling block of his iniquity before his face, and cometh to the prophet; I the Lord will answer him that cometh according to the multitude of his idols." Prayer becomes sinful when you have an idol mounted in your heart. That is, you have made up your mind that you will neither change nor give up on certain things. You have decided not to agree with whoever talks to you on the issue. You might be asked and you would say a grievance is over, but it is still there in your heart. You put your cheque before the Lord, already written out, with the amount already spelt out and now ask Him to sign. You should normally inform Him of your intention before asking Him to sign it.

If you pray with an ambitious mind-set, it is idolatrous. It means you are praying a sinful prayer and the repercussion is so bad that it does not stop at just you who did the praying. It goes down to the generation after you, because prayer is a powerful force. It is not something to be toyed with. When you are asking for the will of God, which He has already made known, you are praying sinful prayers. Balaam went to God asking: "Can I go?" God said, "Don't go." He came the second time, the third and at the fourth time, God said, "Go." We can see what happened to him later.

When you already know the will of God and you are still praying as if you do not, you are in trouble. There was a sister in the '70s, who mocked any brother that proposed marriage to her. She would run them down and say that they were not fit to carry her load. Unfortunately, she still has not found the man that can carry that load. When you have an idol in your heart and pray, you are making a mockery of God and this is sinful. You say you want to get married, and already have someone in mind; in fact, you have started exchanging love letters with the man and both of you are already dreaming of each other. You now start praying to know the will of God, you are making a mockery of Him. You are annoying Him.

2. Praying with one's back to God: Ezekiel 8:16: "And he brought me into the inner court of the Lord's house, and, behold, at the door of the temple of the Lord, between the porch and the altar, were about five and twenty men, with their backs toward the temple of the Lord, and their faces toward the east; and they worshipped the sun toward the east." **Jeremiah 2:27:** "Saying to a stock, Thou art my father; and to a stone, Thou hast brought me forth: for they have turned their back unto me, and not their face: but in the time of their trouble they will say, Arise, and save us."

God did not answer these prayers because they were worshipping other gods. Immediately you have something else you rely upon apart from the Lord, and you start praying to God, it is a sinful prayer. That is, when you show so much love to God with your mouth, and your heart is far from Him, it means you are praying with your back towards Him. When you defile God's clear command and lower His clear standards, do not hope that He will overlook your disobedience. You have turned your back to Him and it is sinful to pray in such an atmosphere.

3. Engaging in public prayer without private communion with God: Matthew 6: 5: "And when thou prayest, thou shalt not be as the hypocrites are: for they love to pray standing in the synagogues and in the corners of the streets, that they may be seen of men. Verily I say unto you, They have their reward." Our Lord denounced the hypocrites who loved to pray for show. When there is little or no private prayer, public prayer becomes sinful.

4. Substituting obedience with prayer: When God gives instructions He demands total obedience. If you are praying about an issue rather than obeying His statutes, the prayer becomes sinful. When you fall into sin, what God expects is repentance, that is, being sorry for what you have done and deciding not to do it again. You may go for deliverance, but it is after genuine repentance that it can be useful otherwise it would be useless. When you pray as a substitute for obedience, that is, God is talking to you and you are not listening, rather you decide to resort to prayer, it will annoy Him because you are taking Him for a ride.

Joshua 7: 10-12: "And the Lord said unto Joshua, Get thee up; wherefore liest thou thus upon thy face? Israel hath sinned, and they have also transgressed my covenant which I commanded them: for they have even taken of the accursed thing, and have also stolen, and dissembled also, and they have put it even among their own stuff. Therefore the children of Israel could not stand before their enemies, but turned their backs before their enemies, because they were accursed: neither will I be with you any more, except ye destroy the accursed from among you." Here, Israel had disobeyed already and the judgment of God was working. Joshua wasted his time praying. God then asked him to get up, and stop praying but should remove the accursed thing. The Bible says that obedience is better than sacrifice.

1 Samuel 15:22-23: "And Samuel said, Hath the Lord as great delight in burnt offerings and sacrifices, as in obeying the voice of the Lord? Behold, to obey is better than sacrifice, and to hearken than the fat of rams. For rebellion is as the sin of witchcraft, and stubbornness is as iniquity and idolatry. Because thou hast rejected the word of the Lord, he hath also rejected thee from being king." Why is obedience better than sacrifice? It is because the Person you are making sacrifice to is already annoyed because He has told you the kind of sacrifice He wants. You cannot bribe God. It should not be so. Prayer cannot substitute for clear obedience to God. Prayer warriors are those who, when God says, "Do this," they would say, "Yes Lord," and will do it, not those who would say, "Yes, but..." When there is disobedience in the camp, in the heart or in the church, it hinders the blessings of God. More prayers would not have been the remedy for Joshua. The great requirement was to get sin out of the camp, not praying.

It is funny to hear somebody speak in tongues and then prophesy to the church, not knowing that what he has said in tongues is not about the church. Some people would sleep and dream and see terrible visions about their own lives but would think they are about their country or church. God could be saying: "You are the city I am referring to." So, if you are praying sinful prayers, desist from it. This is a warning from the Lord.

When you begin to fire your arrows into the camp of the enemy, know that you can revenge all rebellion only when your own obedience is complete. That is, any power rebelling against God in your life or around you, the Bible says you should be ready to avenge it; but you can only do so when your own obedience is complete otherwise, you are wasting your time and the enemies will tell you that you are in the same camp with them. They know that they are God's enemies, but you are like them in your disobedience, so you have become God's enemy too. Before you open your mouth and start singing: "Let God arise and His enemies be scattered," make sure that you are not living in disobedience, for the same disobedience that dealt with Adam and Eve is still dealing with mankind today. There is no new devil, and no new God. They are still the same. The devil has not modernised his methods, they are still the same. Even if what he is doing looks new, it has already been in existence.

5. Selfish prayer: James 4: 3 says, "Ye ask, and receive not, because ye ask amiss, that ye may consume it upon your lusts." The mother of James and John, the sons of Zebedee, asked Jesus to put her sons, one at His right hand and the other at His left, when He gets to the kingdom of God. There were 12 disciples, but the woman wanted her own sons to be on Jesus' either side. Jesus then asked if they could drink the cup that He would drink. They said yes. Of course, they did. James was the first of the disciples to be killed.

Prayer is meant to be God-centred: not self-centred - "me, myself, my wife, my husband, me, me." Balaam prayed all night, but his motive was wrong. If some people were asked to come to church for seven days vigil to pray for the pastors, ministers and the church, they would give excuses. But if you ask them to do the same number of days to pray for prosperity, they would come. In fact, if you ask them to make it

14 days, they will abandon everything and come: and they will not fal asleep. A person who has an interview the next morning is able to pray throughout the night, but if you ask him to pray for new converts, he will sleep off and ask God to keep watch.

6. faithless prayer: A lot of people go to the house of God to pray without expecting much to happen. They go there as if they had gone to gamble. They would say, "Well, maybe I will win one day." No! The Bible says: "He that cometh unto God, must believe that He is, and that He is a rewarder of them that diligently seek Him." But without faith, it is impossible to please God. It is not possible. When the Bible says it is not possible, it means it is not possible. That is, you may be praying but God is not pleased with you because of your level of faith. That is why Jesus got to His hometown and they mocked Him saying: "Jesus, small carpenter, whose brothers and sisters are in our midst here. Miracles? You?" So, He could not do much there and the Bible says: "He marvelled at their unbelief." God was surprised at their unbelief. To pray in unbelief is just as bad as not praying at all (Romans 14:23).

If as the congregation is praying, all of a sudden I begin to prophesy: "You that sister living in one room, the Lord will give you a duplex in a highbrow area of the town, and you will start living there as from tomorrow." The lady concerned may say: "Well, it is the G.O. saying it. I don't know what he saw, but I know right now that I am still owing my landlord six months rent. Maybe it is true that it is God that tells the G.O. this to me." Your inability to instantly believe whatever God tells you is sinful. The Bible calls praying in unbelief, "evil heart of unbelief." It is a sinful prayer. It is a terrible thing to look at a person and conclude that the person can never be good. No, God is an expert in transforming Mr. or Mrs. Nobody to Mr. or Mrs. Somebody. **Psalm 113:7** says: "He raiseth up the poor out of the dust, and lifteth the needy out of the dunghill."

7. Praying to someone instead of to God: Luke 16:24: "And he cried and said, Father Abraham, have mercy on me, and send Lazarus, that he may dip the tip of his finger in water, and cool my tongue; for I am tormented in this flame." He prayed to Abraham instead of praying to God. Of course, the payer was not answered because he was praying to man. Moreover, he was asking for something that Abraham could not handle: only God could have done it. Perhaps you are still praying to virgin Mary, or you are praying with rosary and beads to humans beings like yourself, who lived holy lives. I am sure Mary must be feeling bad in heaven. She was one of those in the Upper Room in Jerusalem to ask for the baptism in the Holy Ghost. Now, men are praying to her as an almighty to help them pray to Jesus. This has no scriptural basis. It is a sinful prayer.

8. Praying out of duty: If you are praying without expecting results but because you have to, it means it is just a religious exercise, a ritual, a routine.

9. Hypocritical praying: Praying lengthy, show-off prayers, so that people will know that you are intelligent, and that you know the Bible and can pray is a sinful prayer. **Matthew 23:14** says, "But woe unto you, scribes and Pharisees, hypocrites! for ye shut up the kingdom of heaven against men: for ye neither go in yourselves, neither suffer ye them that are entering to go in." The way some people pray in public, in a long, self-exalting manner because everybody is listening shows that they are hypocrites.

10. Praying for the ears of men: Matthew 6: 2: "Therefore when thou doest thine alms, do not sound a trumpet before thee, as the hypocrites do in the synagogues and in the streets, that they may have glory of men. Verily I say unto you, They have their reward." **Matthew 16: 5:** "And when his disciples were come to the other side, they had forgotten to take bread." Prayer designed for the ears of men rather than the ears of God is sinful.

---

11. Praying while dodging your responsibility: If you are praying while you know what God has already asked you to do, or you are asking Him to do what He has plainly told you to do for yourself, or you are ignoring the reality of the Scriptures expressed in black and white; you are praying without taking any step to correct the wrongs in your life; you are dodging your personal responsibility instead of repenting and changing decisively; you are asking people to pray for you, assuring them that your anger is leaving you gradually, all these are sinful prayers.

12. Lighting strange fires as prayer: When you change your natural voice during prayers and begin to talk with another voice, you are lighting strange fire before God. Note that there is no professional voice meant for prayers. The Bible says the correct fire will come from the Lord and consume the strange fire that you have lit. Examine the prayer you have been praying, and the heart with which you have been offering it (Romans 8:26). This verse shows us that many prayers say nothing, ask for nothing, expect nothing, and get nothing. The disciples went to Jesus and said, "Lord, teach us to pray" (Luke 11:11). Many people misinterpret this verse to mean "teach us how to pray." They are two different requests. The disciples already knew how to pray, but wanted Him to teach them what to pray. Today, a lot of people know how to pray but don't pray correctly. Many prayers merely bounce off the mouth. If our prayers are to be a force that is difficult for any power to contest, it must follow the biblical pattern. Pray correctly in the spirit, in line with the word of God. When you pray as moved by the Spirit, you pray Spirit-borne prayers guided and empowered by the Holy Spirit. If you continue to pray sinful prayers, they will remain at the human level. Man without the Spirit of God will always pray corrupt prayers. **Romans 8:26** says, "Likewise the Spirit also helpeth our infirmities: for we know not what we should pray for as we ought: but the Spirit itself maketh intercession for us with groanings which cannot be uttered."

You need to allow this revelation in Romans 8:26 to grip your heart and you should go to God and ask Him to teach you to pray, so that the lost art of biblical praying can come back to your life. Sinful prayers don't help anybody. Prayer books are helpful; the beauty is that the prayer points in them are well lined out and targeted. But when you are left on your own with the Lord, what do you pray about? Do you pray satanic prayer points or the ones God wants you to pray?

Some people have prayed that they should die: that the Lord should take them alive. Such people are annoying God because they are blaming Him for creating them. Some secretly wish they were dead. It is a sinful prayer. At this juncture, you need to decide to pray like Apostle John and prophets Daniel and Isaiah, until you can say: "I see the Lord." The day Isaiah saw the Lord, he became a broken man, his ministry changed and he became the messianic prophet. The day Moses encountered God at the burning bush, his destiny changed. You must move to such a realm of prayer.

CHAPTER SIX
ADVANCING YOUR PRAYER LIFE

In this essential topic, the first thing you need to know and agree with is that anything in life that is not making progress will surely die, not only that, the thing would become stagnant and then decay. This principle applies to everything: once a thing is not making any progress, it becomes stagnant, and as a result, decay sets in.

There was a time in Nigeria when you could just go into the bush and ease yourself to your heart's satisfaction, and use a dry leaf to clean up, although your anus would still be smelling. After sometime, there was an advancement: people acquired bowls and instead of going into the bush, they made use of the bowls and in the morning, they got rid of the waste. After a while another means was devised. Big pits were dug into which feaces was passed. As time went on, night-soil men came to the scene. Big round buckets were placed inside the toilet, and once they were filled with feaces, the night-soil men evacuated the waste.

We have moved from this style and advanced to the water closet system. Now, going back to the old system would amount to nothing but timidity, because in everything, there is advancement. Now, there are some toilets where everything inside them work automatically. The closet cleans itself up after every use. That is simply advancement. All these are the replica of what takes place in the spiritual world. In the spirit world, there must be advancement. Some years ago, out of curiosity, I visited my former primary school just to see what it looked like. I entered one of the classrooms and started laughing. Why? The kind of benches they had in the classrooms were so small that I could no longer fit into them. They were so small that no part of my body could go in. It is exactly the same thing in the spirit world. You must move, you must grow and must advance.

Isaiah 16:12 says: "And it shall come to pass, when it is seen that Moab is weary on the high place, that he shall come to his sanctuary to pray; but he shall not prevail." This passage is telling us that even though Moab went to his sanctuary to pray, he would not prevail. It means that his prayers did not go beyond the ceiling. It does not matter whether you go to a mountain in Jerusalem, visit the crying wall, or a mansion built on top of the mountain, once your prayer life is primitive, your prayer will not achieve the desired result.

HOW TO ADVANCE IN YOUR PRAYER LIFE

How do we advance in our prayer life? How do we prevent ourselves from going to the school of Moab? Moab was weary on the high place. He went to his sanctuary to pray but could not prevail.

1. Always make time for prayer: You may never have time to pray if you do not create it. Most people give a lot of excuses about why they cannot pray. We often allow our jobs, household chores and petty businesses to eat up our time. But, anyone that continues with these kinds of excuses, his prayer life will remain rudimentary or at best, primitive. If you want to retain the joy of praying, you have to find time for prayer. The truth is that you can always find time for whatever you want to do, as long as you are serious about it and have made it your priority.

Some people read through the entire pages of newspapers and magazines, including the obituary and advertisement sections, although doing that takes a lot of time. These same people would complain of heavy workload in the office. Some people pray hard before they are promoted but immediately the promotion comes, they forget and relax in prayer, and their prayer life begins to die. They will no longer attend any week meetings in the church. Their brain is always calculating nothing but money. Later, they begin to complain that something is chasing them in the dream. Why not?

The bottom line is this: no matter how busy you are, you can still find time for prayers. Perhaps you need to stop some of your friends from visiting you at night. Perhaps you need to disconnect your television and stereo sets, listen to less music and do more of praying. Perhaps you need to reduce the time you spend on cooking. How will you find time to pray when you spend five hours cooking? You have to pray when you feel like it and when you do not. Nobody was born a prayer warrior. Individuals decide whether to be one or not. But it is unfortunate that many people do not easily want to become prayer warriors. So, God introduces one or two problems here and there to compel them to pray. Once God sees that they have reached the level where they can pray heaven-shaking prayers, He then removes the problems.

2. There is nothing too small to pray about: You must cultivate the habit of praying over everything. Nothing is too small to be prayed about. You have to pray on the shoes, shirts and trousers you put on, and the peppermint you lick on the road. Sometimes, when prayer over such little things are overlooked, they result in big problems. Nothing is too small to be prayed over.

3. Instead of worrying over your problems, pray over them: The more you pray about your challenges, the more God makes a way. The more you receive information on what is really happening, the more you know the mind of God; whether He wants you to stop or proceed. Therefore, instead of worrying over your problems, pray over them.

4. Whenever there is a burden upon your spirit, find out why it came up: There are lots of lonely people in our environment today. They have nobody to talk with. So, they withdraw into themselves and become depressed, unhappy and sad, and soon this leads to their death. This happens because they cannot find out the cause of the burden upon their spirit. As a believer and as one who wants his prayer life to advance, find out very clearly the cause of the burden upon your soul. You may want to ask how this could be done. It is simply by meditation. Meditate upon how that problem got into your spirit: how did it start? How come this problem is bothering me? What kind of dream did I have? What kind of life did I live as an unbeliever? Have I done wrong as a believer and think that nobody saw me? With these facts, you should be able to trace the cause of the burden. Then address it in prayer accordingly.

5. Remove that cause by prayer: The mountain has not been created or built that would stand against warfare prayers, if it is done with a holy heart. So, you can remove whatever is the cause of the burden in your spirit by prayer.

Your life can progress when you learn the principles of removing problems. You must also learn and master the principle known as, "Operation PUSH"- Pray Until Something Happens. Once there is a problem in your spirit and you do not deal with it once and for all, another one would be added to it and they would kill your prayer life as well as suffocate your faith. You may even think that God has gone on holiday, that He is no longer prepared to answer prayers.

6. Make your petition to the Almighty very large: The Bible says, "Open wide your mouth and I will fill it." What does this means? It means you should ask for big things: pray large prayers and God will answer them. The person who prays very little prayers have but little to gain. When others are asking God for multiplication, you should be asking for explosive miracles. When others are asking for motorcycles, you should ask for an aircraft.

7. Keep your tongue from evil: If God is going to use your mouth for prayer then you have to keep your tongue from evil. **Psalm 34: 12-13** says, "What man is he that desireth life, and loveth many days, that he may see good? Keep thy tongue from evil, and thy lips from speaking guile." All prayer warriors who pray to touch heaven are quiet people, not given to rowdiness and noise. It is time for believers to talk only when it is necessary. It is time for all Christians to have the Holy Spirit in their lives before their mouths begin to talk. If you are talkative, your prayer life will never grow, for God does not reveal secrets to human parrots because they will speak when He does not ask them to do so.

8. Link up prayers with violent faith: The Bible says that faith without works is dead. Therefore, you must take an action. River Jordan never parted until the priest stepped into it. Peter could not have walked on the sea if he never got out of the boat. So, it would be with us. Even when God has answered your prayers, if you are not ready to take a step of faith nothing will happen. You are saying: "God, I want to be employed; I need a job," but by 1.00 p.m. you are still on your bed, you do not want to move out or write applications, you want God to write the application letter on your behalf. You are not operating with faith.

9. When you do not feel like praying, that is when you need prayer the most: This is the time when the powers of darkness, who do not want you to confront them hold you hostage. If you allow the enemy to discourage you, and you start wavering and contemplating whether to pray or not, you easily get into trouble.

10. Do not stop praying until you are through: That is what we call pray your way to breakthroughs. Never stop praying until you are through. That is, keep bombarding heaven until God says, "Son or daughter, it's okay, I've heard your prayers. Let's move to another department." Once you have prayed through, you will know and feel it deep down your heart. The Holy Spirit will inform you and you will also know that something definite has happened in the spirit. This is not a job for lazy people.

11. Obtain as many facts as possible on any particular thing you are praying about: Do research work on anything you want from God. Gather as much information and facts as possible and take them to God in prayer. The devil is an expert at making people pray ignorantly. This is why you must gather as many facts as possible on any particular thing you want from God.

12. You must learn the secret of prevailers: What do I mean by this? We know that there are situations where answers to prayers do not come easily. The first thing to prevail over is yourself - you! You may ask how this would be possible. You have to do a lot of work on your own schedule of activities. That is, a situation may arise when you want to pray prevailing prayers, the first thing to do is to prevail over yourself. Since you are the one who has to do the praying, work on your schedule of activities. It may be difficult to find the necessary time for prolonged prayer, but then, you have to adjust your priorities to be able to find that necessary long time.

There is no point in you protesting or comparing yourself with someone else who does not pray as long as you do. Even those who never read the Bible have said that fingers are not equal. You should not use another person's timetable to run your life; you came from different backgrounds and are exposed to different things. One person may pray for two minutes and receive what he wants while another person would have to pray the same prayer for one hour. You must not use someone else as a yardstick for your own life.

You may need to sacrifice some activities in order to give adequate time for your prayer. You have to prevail over yourself to do this. To prevail over yourself, the first thing you have to do is to examine your schedule of activities, remove the ones you know can be removed, and divert the time to prayers. Again, you have to deal with weariness. Some people get weary so easily. The Bible says, "If you faint on the day of adversity your strength is little." When you are saying your prayers, sometimes you may need to take a nap, rise up after a while, and continue. Some people may stop after sometime take some water and continue. After sometime they will find it becoming easier and interesting.

Finally, you need to take the following important decisions to advance your prayer life:

- Henceforth pray much more than you have ever done before. Believers do not usually make new year resolutions, but you can make a vow to the Lord, energised by the Holy Spirit. You can say: "O Lord, from today, I will pray much more than I have ever prayed in the past."
- Pray, whether you feel like praying or not.
- Do all in your power to be filled with the Holy Ghost because once you are filled with the Holy Ghost, praying becomes a thing of joy. In fact, it would become difficult for you to be dragged away from the place of prayer. You may even get upset if disturbed while you are saying your prayers.

Once the spirit of prayer comes upon you, you will not care how much you are sweating, as you are transported to the throne of grace. The Bible says, "Let us come boldly to the throne of grace that we may obtain mercy at the time of need." It also says: "We have a high priest who knows our infirmities, because He has been tested on all fronts."

CHAPTER SEVEN
DOMINION PRAYERS

This concluding topic demands your full attention, and we are going to read some important Scriptures. Let us start with Genesis 1:26-27: "And God said, Let us make man in our image, after our likeness: and let them have dominion over the fish of the sea, and over the fowl of the air, and over the cattle, and over all the earth, and over every creeping thing that creepeth upon the earth. So God created man in his own image, in the image of God created he him; male and female created he them."

According to the above passage, God was not alone when He took the decision to create man. It also says that you and I have the image and likeness of God, even though you may not realise it, and the devil too tries to keep you away from understanding this wonderful mystery. It is still not clear to many people, that the devil actually came to the Garden of Eden to destroy that image and likeness of God, which he once had but lost. Therefore, you need not be surprised when you read the complaints in the book of Romans that the sons of men were waiting for the manifestation of the sons of God; they were waiting for the sons of God to start operating.

There is a mandate in **Jeremiah 1:10** which says: "See, I have this day set thee over the nations and over the kingdoms, to root out, and to pull down, and to destroy, and to throw down, to build, and to plant." What a mandate! So, you were meant to have dominion over kingdoms, to root out, to pull down, and to plant.

All these Scriptures are not for one spiritual giant somewhere. In fact, the Bible says: "Out of the mouth of babes and suckling God has ordained strength." Out of the mouths of those people you do not expect (children), who are there down the ladder, He has ordained strength.

Luke 10: 20 says: "Notwithstanding in this rejoice not, that the spirits are subject unto you; but rather rejoice, because your names are written in heaven." This passage tells us that God reveals things to babes. And who are babes? They are the 'yes men' and 'yes women' for God; those who are completely dependent on God Almighty. These are the kinds of people who can exercise dominion. **1 Corinthians 1:26-29** further tells us the kind of people that are called babes: "For ye see your calling, brethren, how that not many wise men after the flesh, not many mighty, not many noble, are called: But God hath chosen the foolish things of the world to confound the wise; and God hath chosen the weak things of the world to confound the things which are mighty. And base things of the world, and things which are despised, hath God chosen, yea, and things which are not, to bring to nought things that are. That no flesh should glory in his presence."

The apostles of our Lord Jesus were the lowest bunch of people you can think of; fishermen, tax collectors and illiterates. In fact, they were referred to by the people as "unlettered men. But these men turned the world upside down and left it confounded. **Ecclesiastes 9:11** says: "I returned, and saw under the sun, that the race is not to the swift, nor the battle to the strong, neither yet bread to the wise, nor yet riches to men of understanding, nor yet favour to men of skill; but time and chance happeneth to them all." The fact that you are told to get on your marks, get set, and go, and you happen to be the first fellow to dash forward, does not mean that you will win the race. The battle of life is like that. The fact that you are big, mighty and strong does not qualify you to exercise the power of God.

WHAT IS DOMINION?

The word dominion is derived from the Latin word 'dominus,' which means lord and master. What does it mean to have dominion? It means to dominate. And what does it mean to dominate? It means to control, to rule by strength or power, to prevail over, to rise high above, to govern and to hold a commanding position over something.

WHAT IS DOMINION PRAYER?

- Dominion prayer is the prayer to dominate.
- Dominion prayer is a prayer to exercise authority over every problem and negative opposition. When somebody prays and says, "I take authority over you sickness," that fellow is praying a dominion prayer. When somebody says, "Surrender and be subdued," he is praying a dominion prayer.

Dominion prayer is a prayer to show who is the boss.

During a deliverance session at MFM Port Harcourt one particular morning, pandemonium suddenly broke out: everyone ran in different directions. A girl was being prayed for. And while she lied helplessly on the floor, two serpents came out from her body. Even the people who brought the girl saw the snakes and ran away. But the deliverance ministers moved in and were able to kill one of the snakes while the other one ran into the bush. The one that was killed was burnt to ashes. Members of the congregation did not wait for the deliverance session to end before they ran into town and spread the news about the snakes. People began to rush to the church. What really happened there was that somebody prayed a dominion prayer and the serpents had to come out. They were dominating an environment before, but when a higher and greater power came on the scene, they came out.

- Dominion prayer is prayer to disobey counterfeit command. When a voice says, "Okay, you were diagnosed as not having enough blood in your system, therefore, remain on that sick bed." That is an evil command. But when you disagree and jump up from that bed, that is dominion prayer.

- Dominion prayer is prayer to undo the works of darkness. When the enemies have already packaged their evil and you begin to unpack it, that is dominion prayer.

- Dominion prayer is a prayer to silence the angels of the spirit of death. When you say, "You spirit of death, lose your hold, in the name of Jesus," you are praying dominion prayer.

- Dominion prayer is a prayer to dethrone false kings.

- Dominion prayer is a prayer to take your rightful position. When you say: "Sorry, I am not supposed to be here, I am supposed to be in that position, and I claim it by fire," you are praying dominion prayer.

- Dominion prayer is a prayer to address the earth and the seas. You are praying dominion prayer when you say, "You earth, vomit my portion." Without dominion prayers what power has a man got to be able to stand against the earth? You are also praying dominion prayer when you say: "You sea, vomit my portion and disobey any negative instruction against me, being passed to you." This is simply taking authority.

- Dominion prayer is a prayer to address the heavenly– the sun, moon and stars. You are praying dominion prayer when you say: "You this day, reject every enchantment against me."

- Dominion prayer is a prayer to address the elements – the wind, fire, rain, lightening, thunder, earthquake, air and the likes of them. These are the kinds of prayers prophet Elijah prayed in those days. Imagine a tiny man sitting down here on earth and issuing command that it should not rain. That was dominion prayer.

- Dominion prayer is a prayer to force evil powers to vomit what they have swallowed.

Sometime ago, we went to pray for someone who was at the point of death. As the prayer went on, I found that the enemies had already eaten the head and one arm of this fellow. All that were left were one arm, two legs and the rest of the body, which were being gradually eaten by these powers. Then we began to pray dominion prayers. We asked these evil powers to vomit what they had eaten from this person. Of course, they had had their lunch and gone away. One of them could have been in India, while the rest were scattered to places like Port Harcourt, Zaria, or even America. They all had to come and vomit every part of the flesh they had eaten. This was a dominion prayer.

- Dominion prayer is a prayer to force wicked powers to drink their own blood and eat their own flesh. You can find this in the Bible. In the popular Isaiah 49:26, God promises to feed our enemies with their own flesh and make them drunken with their own blood as with sweet wine. Therefore, prayers to force your enemies to eat their flesh and drink their own blood are dominion prayers.

- Dominion prayer is a prayer to command inanimate things to cooperate with you.

- Dominion prayer is a prayer to destabilise reluctant and stubborn enemies.

- Dominion prayer is a prayer to force the powers of darkness to carry out your orders.

In the Bible, some spirits told Jesus not to send them out of the body of a person they were inhabiting because they knew that they had to comply once He issued the order. Therefore, they tried to dissuade Him from issuing the command. It is like the story of the brother who just returned from a crusade, entered his bedroom and found that the chairs had gone elsewhere and every other item in the bedroom had changed position. Right there, he saw a demon smiling at a corner of the room. He got mad and addressed the demon like this: "You devil, when I left this place, my bed was in that corner of the room, the chairs and other items were not where they are now. Therefore, I command you to rearrange these items to their former positions, in Jesus' name." Immediately, the demon that was smiling a while ago stopped smiling and began to rearrange the items as commanded by the brother. That was dominion prayer.

- Dominion prayer is a prayer to summon your enemies to the court for prosecution. You can say, "Every spirit behind my case, come out right here and now. I have controversy against you."
- Dominion prayer is a prayer to issue judgement as it is written in Psalm 149. The Bible says that no weapon formed against you shall prosper, and every tongue that rises against you in judgement shall be condemned.
- Dominion prayer is a prayer to arrest satanic soldiers and policemen.
- Dominion prayer is a prayer to demand restitution from spiritual thieves.
- When a person says, 'I claim seven-fold restitution from satan,' he is praying dominion prayers.
- Dominion prayer is a prayer to torture demons with the blood of Jesus.
- Dominion prayer is a prayer to be the head and not the tail, to be above only and not beneath. God Almighty has already ordained that His children shall always be above only. But that has to be enforced through a prayer pattern known as dominion praying.
- Dominion prayer is a prayer to control obstinate and, or stubborn authorities, and even individuals.

Dominion prayer is a prayer to command satan to restrain his agents.

Dominion prayer is a prayer to divert evil arrows.

If arrows are coming to you, you can say, "No, just change your direction." This is dominion prayer.

In these last days, our prayers must change as things are no longer as easy as they used to be. Things are not as straightforward as they used to be. The words in the book of Revelation are coming to pass, that evil men shall wax stronger and stronger. The words of the gospel have come to pass, that the love of many shall wax cold. The words of the Scriptures have come to pass that the enemy has come down with great wrath, knowing that he has a short time. Beloved, we need to pray dominion prayers.

WHY DOMINION PRAYERS?

❖ *The enemy is wicked:* The key ingredient of satan's attack is wickedness. And the Bible makes us to understand that there are variations of wickedness in the satanic kingdom. Mathew 12:43-45 tells us that when an unclean spirit leaves a man, it does not go far but moves about, watching the place where it came out from whether it is swept, empty and garnished. And if it is so, it now gets seven spirits more wicked than itself to re-inhabit that place. And the Bible concludes that the end of that fellow shall be worse.

If you pinch a person, it is wickedness. But that level of wickedness is different from when you slap him. And biting differs from a slap. Even biting has different levels. I have seen somebody's ear bitten off completely. When we talk about beating, there is a great difference between a fellow who uses bathroom slippers to hit you and another who makes use of a wooden cane. A fellow who pours ground pepper on a person does him very little harm compared to another who pours acid on him.

I have seen a person whose limbs were cut off. That is wickedness. Once I was watching a documentary on the war in Sierra Leone, some innocent people's limbs were cut off because they did not support a particular group. It is also wickedness to cut off a person's hand and legs. A man had his penis cut off in Kano, Nigeria. There are different levels of wickedness. Wickedness is defined as something that is highly injurious and, or destructive in character. If you leave room for your enemy, he will strike and destroy you. This is one of the reasons we need dominion prayers.

❖ *The enemy can sometimes be stubborn and reluctant.*
❖ *The enemies are extremely quick and intelligent.* If they try a method on somebody and find that it does not work, they change their style.
❖ *Our enemies move and relay information at incredible speed.*
❖ *They can decide to be deaf and dumb.*
❖ *They can use the spirit of dead human beings to attack the living.*
❖ *They can travel within seconds or minutes from one side of the world to another to interfere with deliverance sessions.* We were praying for a woman in Kaduna and at a point she stood up like a soldier and said in Yoruba dialect: "Eyin egbe mi da?" meaning, where are my colleagues? She was inviting some spirits to come. At another occasion, we were praying for a person and another fellow came from the back and joined hands with the person that was being delivered to support the latter.
❖ *Evil powers tormenting a fellow could be reporting to a bigger and stronger boss.* This means that the demon spirits possessing a person can go out, report to a bigger and superior demon and return again. That is why some people can have a temporary relief only for the problem to come back.
Every individual who poses a serious threat to the kingdom of darkness or that God can use becomes a serious target for the enemy.
❖ *A lot of people are at various levels of spiritual bondage.*

SAMPLE PRAYER POINTS

We have seen so much on the theoretical part of this message. We have been able to give some facts on the subject of dominion prayers. Let us look at what I call 'sample prayer points.' These prayer points would have catastrophic effects on the enemy. They are all dominion prayers.

• *Ask the enemies to go to the pit before their time*: The enemies do not like this kind of prayer at all. For example, when you

80

say, "You spirit of poverty, release me and go to the pit before your time." They do not like it at all. They would rather prefer that you say, "Go out," so that they would look for another candidate. Some people do not understand the kind of prayers we pray in MFM. For example, if a fellow prays that a spirit should fall down and die, the person is simply saying that the spirit should go to the pit before its time. When you say 'die' to a human being, it means something different. It means that the person should cease to breath, that his spirit should leave his body. But when you say die to a spirit, it is another thing entirely. What you are telling the spirit to do is to go to the pit before it's time and to become completely unavailable. They are afraid of this kind of prayer points and do not like people praying them. At Mountain of Fire and Miracles Ministries, we do not pray that human beings should fall down and die, but the spirit behind their problem, as I earlier emphasized. These demons do protest. They do not like such prayers. In the Scriptures, we read that they begged Jesus, "Please, Sir, do not send us to that place." They did not want to go. They said, "Have you come to torment us before our time? We know who you are." It means that demons have time to deal with people and destroy them. But when you now say, "Go before your time," they will be in trouble.

- *Ask the evil spirits to come out with all their roots.*
- *Render them homeless by fire.* You can cause a great trouble for them with this prayer because they do not like losing their accommodation. That was why they referred to human body as their home.
- *Ask them to receive spiritual starvation.* When you say this, the demons would be hungry. They would have no blood to drink and no flesh to eat. It is a terrible command.
- *Command them to receive triangular attack from the Father, the Son and the Holy Spirit.* This is an attack with no room of escape.
Tell them to eat their own flesh and drink their own blood.

You can pray thus:
-	You messenger of death, you must die in my place after the order of Haman, in the name of Jesus.

81

- O cauldron of darkness, revolt and capture your owner now, in the name of Jesus.
- Let the weapons of the enemy backfire, in the name of Jesus.
- I cause civil war in the kingdom of darkness, in the name of Jesus.

BROKENNESS: THE KEY TO DOMINION PRAYERS

It is possible to pray these prayers and the enemy counters you. This is just because you lack a required element – brokenness. For you to pray dominion prayers and it works for you like fire, there is only one key, and this is where many people have problem. It is unfortunate that a lot of people who attend churches these days are not broken yet. Some do not even know where they are, and are still roaming about with their second and third wives. Some are still playing with fornication and adultery. Some still spread rumours and backbite while some are still busy uttering slander. It is simply because they are not broken. The same mouth with which you gossip, or curse and abuse people, if you now use it to say: "You cauldron of darkness, revolt," they would not answer. Rather, they would charge back in anger and say, "You know you are one of us? The only difference is that you do not have a pot yet. You are one of us because you gossip and tell lies and you are still issuing us command. Sorry, you cannot command us because we are in you." The kind of life that many people are living in these last days is the life of silent sin. This has paralysed and is still paralysing so many modern-day Christians. Many harbour the deposits and anointing of hell fire inside their lives. Many have things planted in their lives that are moving them closer to hell fire than to God. How can you be binding and loosing when you are just by the edge of hell fire? That is why people with closed minds, who come to the house of God are unteachable. When you ask them: "Please, be quiet!" that is when they start speaking more. When you say: "Let us open to the book of Deuteronomy," they would be opening the book of Revelation. Sometimes, some sisters chew gum on their way to church and their heads are not covered, except for a tiny handkerchief they place on their heads. At times I wonder and say: "Where are these ones going? To the church or elsewhere?" They do not understand. Some would even come to church in trousers. They want to pray but hate the discipline that goes with it.

A sister once told me that she does not like the 'church look'. This means that there is another 'look' that is not 'church.' However, I regret to tell those who are not broken that they are wasting time in the church. The more you pray those prayers while you are not broken, the more you are looking for trouble.

Some people behave very badly and it does not prick their conscience. This is part of what I have been talking about- 'rebellion.' When there is no godly sorrow for sin, it means there is no brokenness in the life of the fellow. You commit sin and not feel sorry about it, this is the reason many people pray and there is no answer. How can it work when you have no godly sorrow for your sin. Many are not sensitive to their own spiritual weakness. Some have their own special seats, and any other person who sits there is in trouble. This is unbrokenness of the highest order. There are people with hard hearts, the kind of hard hearts that even God is finding difficult to penetrate. Such people are also shaking and binding and loosing demons. No, somebody must tell you the truth that you are wasting time. The earlier you begin to live a broken life, the better. The Spirit of God came like a dove upon Jesus. He was a lamb. The dove will only descend on lambs and not on goats.

All the quiet disobedience to God is rebellion. God says, "Go and give testimony." But you say, "No, I am shy." This is pride despite the fact that you promised God that you would give testimony. All forms of hypocrisy, pride, and unloving character are acts of unbrokenness.

In these last days we are working against clever enemies. You have to be more serious with your Christian life so that you can pray and the prayer will have some impact. The Bible says, "The effectual, fervent prayer of a righteous man availeth much." It means that prayer has to be effectual, that is, have impact.

Do you want your prayers to avail? Then you must be broken. All the sample prayer points that I have mentioned are good foundation on which we can stand.

Made in the USA
Monee, IL
17 March 2022

93064298R00049